DRIED FLOWERS

DRIED FLOWERS

MARIE VAN DEN BERK-MERTENS

WARD LOCK LIMITED · LONDON

© Uitgeverij Cantecleer bv, de Bilt 1979

© English translation Ward Lock Limited 1987

First published in Holland as *Een Boeket vol droogbloemen* by Cantecleer bv
de Bilt

First published in Great Britain in 1987
by Ward Lock Limited, 8 Clifford Street
London W1X 1RB, an Egmont Company

Text filmset/set in Bodoni
by Tradespools Ltd, Frome

Printed and bound in Italy
by Sagdos

British Library Cataloguing in Publication Data

Berk-Mertens, Marie van den
Dried flowers
1. Flowers—Drying
I. Title   II. Een boeket vol droogbloemen.
English
745.92   SB447

ISBN 0-7063-6559-3

CONTENTS

FOREWORD

The first snow of 1979 fell on New Year's Eve and ushered in a winter that will not be forgotten for many years. The sounds from outside became quieter and quieter, while indoors the light took on a strange whiteness. A sense of isolation came over our village reminiscent of war-time. The snow-covered world crippled social contact, and again it was brought home to us that even today man is still powerless before the forces of nature. Most of northern Europe struggled arduously through this barren period.

What was lying asleep under that carpet of white? Where were the hedgehogs, the squirrels, the lizards, and all the insects? Where were the millions of seeds and plants hidden below it? The snow lay so long that it seemed as if the world would never again turn green. Only the hellebore or Christmas rose, with its warm-yellow stamens, showed something of the hidden powers of growth.

Out of nostalgia for the summer we gathered together our stock of colourful dried flowers, for in the same way that as children we made autumn collections of chestnuts, nuts and apples, so too each year we lay by a stock of floral delights. Man does not live by bread alone, and plants and flowers are a good counterbalance to a too-technical and over-commercialized world. One or two friends also began to collect their own flowers and dry them and in doing so they started to exchange various items.

It is worth noting here that the many kinds of flowers that can be dried have different names in different countries; but even if a few liberties have been taken, normally people find that they can understand what is meant in this area.

I should like to extend my thanks to a number of people who have given their help and support: Henny van Bommel-Meusen of Venlo, who devoted herself particularly to creating a number of delightful flights of fancy using natural products and her own creations. Truus Kersten-Houtackers of Haelen, who incorporated into a refined palette of rust, grey-green and yellow flowers, herbs and seed heads which she grew herself. Neel Luyten-Simons of Grathem, who gave us practical advice. Ingrid Nijssen-Visser of Asselt who used wild material to produce arrangements in natural and pastel tints with romantic backgrounds. Most of the dried flower plants used were grown for us by Messrs Piet Korten of Olier, Mathieu Moons of Neeritter and Martin Timmermans now of Limbricht.

Special mention must be made of Hans van Ommeren, the dedicated photographer from Woerden who peered through the lens for hours to create a harmonious record of everything, thereby making an essential contribution to the book.

Marie van den Berk-Mertens
Grathem Spring 1979

INTRODUCTION

Since the very earliest of times, flowers have been highly valued for their beauty and fragrance. Moreover, all types of plants, and representations of them, have always played an important part in people's lives, whether as decoration, for medicinal purposes or as religious symbols.

The paradise story in Genesis tells of the Garden of Eden, a place of delights that could be called the oldest garden of all. With the rise of the first great empires in human civilization, Babylon, Egypt, China and Mexico, the first artificially cultivated plants also came into being. Even in those times men were undaunted by technical difficulties, for as early as 3000 BC gardens were laid out in the heart of the desert, in remote and dry locations. Palm trees were used to protect the tender plants from the fierce sun and at the same time their fruits could be enjoyed and their fibres used for weaving.

Babylon was famed for its hanging gardens, laid out on flat roofs which ran downhill in terraces. Hollow tree trunks were filled with soil to form natural pots for shrubs and flowers. According to the records, the impression gained by visitors approaching from a distance was that the whole of this exotic plant world was suspended from the dome of heaven. The Egyptians also cultivated flowers. Ancient frescoes show pools of water lilies, and peasants weeding among flowers and grapes.

The Chinese used to decorate their interiors with peonies, chrysanthemums, marigolds, tulips, and thousands of other kinds of flowers. Oil of roses was obtained from the damask rose, and people always carried various scented waters on their person. So attached to their flowers were the ancient Chinese that they often took a miniature garden with them on their travels.

In Japan, cherry blossom was the favourite, and many centuries later it can still be seen on black lacquered trays and black porcelain tea services, the decorative white blossom providing a beautiful contrast. This popular flower also still blooms on Japanese ladies' slippers and kimonos.

The Germans, practical then as now, divided their gardens into two sections, one for useful plants and one for flowers. Around the flower beds there were palings painted in the family colours. Flower species are represented on many coats of arms.

Castle gardens naturally set the style, and it was there that people began to give nature a helping hand. In Italy box hedges were laid out, into which 'windows' were cut to give surprising prospects and glimpses of what lay beyond. Box trees, and later also beech hedges, were trimmed into shape to provide not only garden vases in living greenery but also birds, beasts and even representations of mathematical models.

In France it became the fashion to grow beds of flowers in such a way that they gave the impression of having been made not using rake and trowel but using an embroidery needle, with all the flowers at the same

height and in harmonious colours. Appropriately enough, people called them 'embroidery beds'.

Since Moslems are forbidden to depict human or animal forms, their mosques are richly decorated with stylized flowers and plants, motifs which are also to be found in Arab and Persian carpets. In folklore numerous plants and flowers have sagas and legends attaching to them, whilst many personal names derive from flowers.

The role of flowers and plants was not restricted to decoration. From olden times herbs were extensively collected for use in medicine, and they were also closely connected with resisting evil spirits. In ancient Greece a dried laurel branch was hung on each house as a protection against demons. When Odysseus and his comrades were bewitched by the angry Circe, only the herb Moly could bring deliverance. This is why flowers also play a part in religion. Byzantine icons often depict a graceful green leaf, usually the holm-oak. St Joseph's staff bloomed with a profusion of white lilies on the morning when he was chosen by Mary. His companions broke their own walking staves in displeasure. On sarcophagi one finds garlands and rosettes carved in stone. Stained glass windows and tapestries are often filled with scenes rich in colourful flowers. With endless patience, the monks decorated old liturgical books and manuscripts in such minute detail that even the brilliant azure speedwell can be distinguished in the miniatures. On Renaissance tapestries one can see meadows sown with flowers worked so meticulously that even the veins of the leaves can be made out. People took such tapestries with them on journeys, and they were then embroidered with as many kinds of flower as possible, the so-called 'millefleurs'.

But at bleak times of the year when it was necessary to stay indoors, yet when people did not want to be without flowers, they would enjoy the representation of flowers, woven on great tapestries. Painters were commissioned to reproduce nature's riches on canvas. To do so they even made their paint out of natural raw materials. St John's Wort, lichen, dyer's broom, onions, madder, ferns and heather provided delightful hues which were applied using white of egg. However, one of the best ways of all to capture the beauty of flowers and plants permanently is to use them dried. The unique colours and textures – rich yet subtle – of dried flowers makes it possible to use them to create wonderful decorative displays, both formal and informal. And they provide the opportunity for you to give full rein to your creative abilities.

Opposite Variations on the colour white. There is no reason why you shouldn't choose white for a one-colour arrangement: this one is a harmonious display of white, cream, gold and beads. Don't forget that even the smallest details are important: here the oval oasis is hidden behind the white lawn used to line the basket. Against a background of white statice we see Cape white, roses, catsfoot, fine white hebe Armstrongii, and cream-coloured immortelles. This arrangement is filled out with artificial flowers: silk and gold brocade roses, bead flowers and thin balsa-wood roses. All these have been combined into a large, spacious oval arrangement.

1 DRYING TECHNIQUES

Summer is the best time for gathering material. Pick the flowers just before they are fully open, and preferably on a warm day. It is rather cruel to plunder the plants before they are in full bloom, but they will last longer. Seeds should be harvested when they are on the point of dropping off. Roots should be taken from the ground in the autumn. Almost any flower can be dried, but you will need access to a dry place, for example an attic, a cupboard that can be left ajar, a dry shed, or above a radiator. It is important that there is adequate ventilation so that moisture can escape quickly. In addition, the drying process should preferably take place in the dark so that the colours do not fade. Each species demands its own treatment, of course, but in general flowers need from four to fourteen days to dry properly. Flowers dry more slowly than grasses, which by their nature are already somewhat drier.

There are various drying methods:
  i) Drying in air.
  ii) Pressing in a flower press or book.
  iii) Drying in a tin using borax, silica gel, silver sand, washing powder or sieved shell-lime.
  iv) Preserving by placing in a mixture of glycerine and water in a jar or bowl.
  v) Some kinds can be picked when dry, after nature has already started the process.
  vi) Rapid drying in the oven.
  vii) Ironing dry, using a flat-iron.

DRYING IN AIR

The flowers should be picked or purchased on a dry day, so that there is less moisture to evaporate. The stamens must be upright, the foliage still in perfect condition and the colours bright. If the plants have been pollinated by the bees, the colours tend to lose some of their clarity and sometimes, as in the case of viper's bugloss, the colour will actually change.

Strip off the leaves. Gather the stems into bunches and hold with a rubber band. Do not make the bunches too big. Double the rubber band around the bunch to form a loop by which the bunch can be hung up (fig. 1). From time to time tighten the ties as the flowers tend to shrink. Do not hang the bunches too close together, as air must circulate between them to prevent mould developing. Also, hang them in a dark place in order to preserve the colours.

Large flowers that bloom in clusters, such as hydrangeas (which should be picked when they are fading) should first be placed in a vase containing about 5 cm (2 in) of water. As soon as the water has evaporated the flowers are hung up to dry. This is always successful.

All everlasting flowers can be dried hanging up; they have a high wood content, with correspondingly little moisture. They include all species of *helichrysum, lonas, anaphalis*, statice (*limonium*), cupid's dart (*catananche*), (*xeranthemum*), yarrow (*achillea*), *helipterum*, edelweiss and thistles.

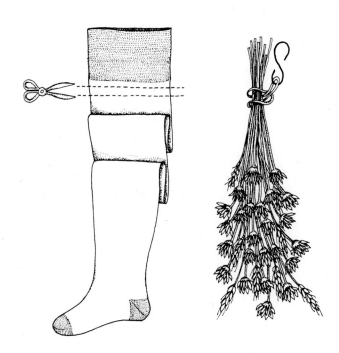

1 Drying flowers in the air: gather into bunches and hold together with a rubber band (right); alternatively, cut a loop from an old stocking (left). Hang the bunches up with hooks made by bending thin steel wire.

PRESSING FLOWERS

The flowers should be picked and placed in the press before they wilt; in other words as soon as possible. Flower presses can be bought, but you can also make one quite inexpensively, using two thick seets of plywood or hardboard with a wing-nut at each corner (fig. 3). The flowers will be dry in a week. Plenty of absorbent material must be used, otherwise the flower will decay and brown spots form. Sheets of kitchen roll, white blotting paper or toilet paper are very serviceable. The paper must not have a raised pattern on it, or this will

become imprinted on the petals. It is sometimes advisable to use a little naphthaline to guard against mould. Of course, the flowers can also be slipped between the pages of a sufficiently heavy book. Violets, pansies, daisies, primulas, hollyhocks, cow parsley, wild carrot and so on, which have thick centres, should be laid between sheets of paper folded into four, into the middle of which a small hole has been cut to make room for the flower centre (fig 2). When the flower has been placed in position it is again covered with absorbent paper.

When you are on a journey you can collect souvenirs by pressing the plucked flowers between the pages of a substantial book, putting a heavy suitcase on top of it, or if necessary sitting on the book. Sheets of newspaper are

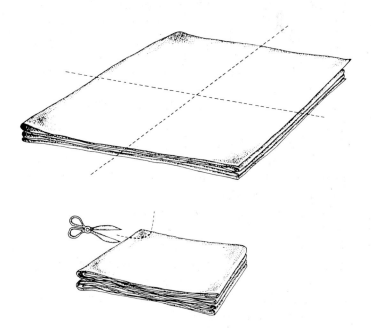

2 How to fold a sheet of paper for pressing flowers. Fold into four. Cut a semi-circle from one corner. This will produce a hole in the middle of the paper to make room for a thick flower centre.

particularly suitable to lay the picked flowers between, as mould does not like the smell of printing ink. It is not a good idea to peep at the results too soon, for if the flowers move, the petals can become wrinkled and there is no way of correcting this.

If you are so impatient that you need to ask Interflora to deliver a bit of parsley to your door then you should forget flower pressing. Delicate flowers especially, such as African violets, hollyhocks and foxgloves, are of a silk-like thinness and require a certain amount of care and time. If you really want to see rapid results, the flowers can be ironed dry using a cool iron. The flowers should be ironed between blotting paper and then stored in a book. This gives very good results with the species just mentioned. Bell-shaped flowers such as, for example, the foxglove, should first be cut open and carefully opened out; on drying they show delightful shapes that resemble Charleston dresses.

Obviously pressed flowers can only be used on flat surfaces, but it is a good way of compiling a library of flowers. It is also a suitable method for drying leaves. Ferns, oak leaves and even rhubarb show up their mesophylls – that is, the inner tissues of the leaves – in delightful tints. The delicate feathery leaves of mimosa, which are dark green, also produce a very decorative

Opposite The flowers in the box are carnations and gerberas (a kind of large daisy). The blue silica gel in the white, oval dish will be sprinkled over these to preserve them. The blue pool at the Madonna's feet on the lid of the box changes colour with the humidity: the blue shows that the room is centrally heated and therefore dry. On the large sheet of paper in the centre are dried pressed flowers which are to be made into a picture like the one above the sheet. The dark-coloured bowl on the left is an arrangement based on dried weeds and seeds: milfoil, tansy, stonecrop, dill, lonas or yellow ageratum, St John's wort and wild carrot give this arrangement its beautiful muted tones.

effect. It is best to use tweezers when handling material of this kind.

Fabric glue should be used to create arrangements using your pressed flowers. Some kinds of glue leave stains, so experiment first. You are recommended to have a wet cloth handy to keep your hands and materials clean.

In the photograph opposite there is a bouquet of pressed flowers on paper in the background. The mauve part round the edges is made from dried hollyhocks. An arrangement like this should be carefully put in place before any of the pieces are glued down. The centre is filled in with violets interspersed with a few blue hydrangeas and some yellow and reddish-brown gazanias. The stems at the bottom are made from a bunch of lavender or thin immortelles.

Making a press
A small press can be made from two pieces of hardboard 19 cm (7½ in) square, between which are sheets of corrugated cardboard and paper or blotting paper, so that the pressure is evenly distributed. Make a hole at each of the four corners, and tighten the press by means of a wing-nut in each corner (fig. 3). To dry large flowers, make a similar press, 30 cm (12 in) square. The flowers will then have more room, for they must not be allowed to touch each other.

Flowers that do not do so well in vases, for example Christmas roses, (*helleborus*), African violets and hollyhocks, are ideal subjects for drying flat. For thick flowers it is necessary first to tighten the press lightly, tightening further after a day or two, and only after that tightening it to its full extent. These flat subjects can be used for Christmas and New Year cards, on menus, under glass on a serving tray, as window decorations, in old frames, or glued onto lampshades. You can keep your stock of flowers in an album arranged by seasons.

17

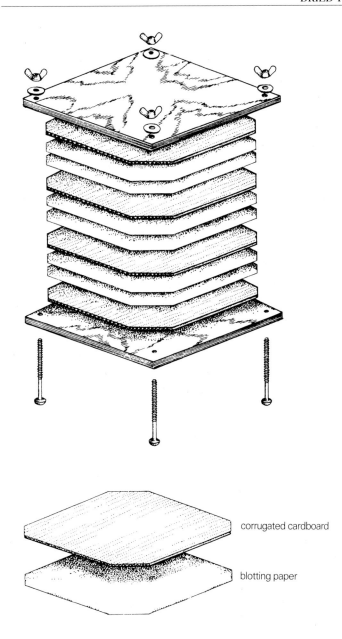

corrugated cardboard

blotting paper

3 A flower press with alternate layers of corrugated cardboard and kitchen paper between which the flowers can be dried.

DRYING IN A TIN

The drum is partly filled with one of the drying agents mentioned earlier. Silica gel consists of crystals which are hygroscopic; that is, they take up water from their surroundings. The crystals are blue when dry, gradually turning pink as they take up moisture, which is why silica gel is used in all manner of weather-forecasting devices. The crystals are small and light and so do not damage the flowers, and as soon as they have changed colour as a result of taking up moisture they can be restored to their original state by putting them on a tray in a moderate oven.

To use, first cover the bottom of the tin with a thin layer of crystals. Lay the flowers on this with their heads downwards, then carefully pour the rest of the silica gel crystals over them until everything is covered, making sure that the crystals go between all the petals of the flowers. Close the tin firmly and put it away in a dry place. Ideally the lid should be sealed using adhesive tape so that no fresh air can get in. Even with silica gel the flowers will fade a little, but the delicate tints have a charm all their own. The drying time depends on many factors. Violets dry in three days. Zinnias are very quick because they are already fairly dry, and are completely open. Large flowers require more time; dahlias and chrysanthemums are difficult because of their thickness and their closed forms. Remember that after drying, the stems will be very brittle, but they can be strengthened beforehand using rose wire (fig. 4).

Silica gel is the most expensive of the various drying agents, but it lasts for years and gives the best results. It can be obtained from a chemist.

PRESERVING IN GLYCERINE

Glycerine is a sticky, greasy liquid. (It should *not* be swallowed). Place the flowers in a mixture of two parts of boiling water to one part of glycerine. The stems should have been standing in warm water for a few hours. In both cases the liquid level must be sufficiently high, preferably at least 10 cm (4 in). Stems which contain a lot of wood, such as lilacs, magnolias, hydrangeas or oak twigs must be split beforehand. Make a cut about 5 cm (2 in) long using a sharp knife. Again the drying times are very variable. During drying it is best to put the whole pot and its contents into an empty bucket so that the stems still have some support. Glycerine is suitable for drying autumn cuttings and creepers, and brides' bouquets. The leaves become supple and fade. When they are taken out of the mixture they should be left hanging upside down for a few days longer, so that the glycerine can penetrate to the very tips of the flowers. The water in the capillaries has now been replaced by glycerine and this is what makes the plants supple.

DRIED BY NATURE

These are the easiest and therefore often the most gratifying for the beginner to experiment with. The flowers need only to be hung up in the dark until you are ready to arrange them. To name just a few: poppies, lavender, gypsophila, tansy, and others too numerous to mention. Nature itself dries a great many plants, and when making dried bouquets we do not need to restrict ourselves to one or two flowers.

RAPID DRYING IN THE OVEN

This is good for leaves that are not over-large. The method is to put them on a tray and place them in an oven – which must not of course be too hot – carefully rearranging or repositioning everything from time to time. The technique is identical to the old-fashioned way of drying fruit, when people used to dry thin slices of apples and pears. The faster the moisture disappears the better the result, but for this very reason the method cannot be used for drying large flowers.

Herbs such as parsley, celery, thyme, marjoram, dill, mint, chervil, savory and so on can also be dried in the oven. First put them into boiling water in which a good handful of salt has been dissolved. Let them drain and then dry them for a quarter of an hour in a preheated oven. Leave the oven door open. Rub the herbs and store them away for future use.

2 EQUIPMENT FOR DRYING

TOOLS AND MATERIALS

Before dried flower arrangements can be made up, there are a number of basic tools and materials that will be needed.

Absorbent paper Blotting paper, toilet paper or a piece of kitchen roll will readily absorb moisture and this makes them very useful for drying flowers that have large centres or fairly thick blooms.

Floral tape This is used to hide the stems and wire. It is obtainable in various colours and widths.

Flower press This will be useful for drying flowers flat. These presses can be bought. For larger flowers it is simple to make your own (see page 17).

Flower spray Before they can be used, some flowers, seeds and mosses need to be moistened using a flower spray.

Bread knife It is a good idea to use a bread knife to cut pieces of styrofoam or oasis to shape.

Plasticine, double fix or self hardening clay are used to secure elements in an arrangement, for example a candle in a holder.

Drying powders and drying crystals Silica gel (crystals), washing powders, borax and ground shell-lime for preserving flowers in their natural (three-dimensional) shapes (see page 18).

Glycerine is used to conserve woody plants (see page 18). It is supplied by most chemists.

Nylon or rubber bands Nylon loops can be cut from old nylon stockings (fig.1). These loops are very useful for hanging up small bunches of flowers. A rubber band can also be used for this.

Tweezers are handy for picking up dried flowers, as they are very delicate.

Rose wire and/or steel wire is obtainable in various thicknesses. The most common ones are 0.4mm (for delicate materials and for working with gold wire, see fig 26, page 72); 0.8mm (for heavier materials and for hooks to hang flowers up by, see pages 14–15); 1mm (as support in a plait).

Scissors and knife You will need a sharp potato knife for gathering and arranging flowers. You should always have a pair of scissors handy for cutting flower stems, gold foil, adhesive tape, paper, string etc.

Oasis In arrangements the flowers are inserted into an oasis. The most widely used and best known is the green oasis. Most delicate flowers can be inserted into it. For heavier flowers styrofoam provides more stable support. Both materials can be obtained in sheets, blocks, balls, cones and wreaths.

Opposite *The hydrangeas have been dried in a glycerine solution and then broken into pieces and made into bundles of different colours on a piece of wire. To add variety, a dried rose, some small* xerantherum *and pink or blue panited* anaphalis *have been added. The velvet ribbons give the arrangement the distinctive look of a Victorian posy.*

Pincers You will need a small pair of pincers for cutting wire and bending it to shape.

Fabric glue We use fabric glue to stick flowers on to flat backgrounds. Keep a moist cloth handy to wipe off any glue marks straight away.

Tins Any tin with an airtight lid can be used as a drying tin when you are working with silica gel.

Paint Various kinds of paint can be used when working with dried flowers. Paint in spray cans is the most convenient, but is fairly expensive. Paint can also be applied using an artist's brush. A third option is to dye flowers in fabric dye.

DYEING PLANTS AND FLOWERS

Dried flowers, grasses and grains are easy to dye. On the stove, bring a dessertspoon of dye (textile, egg or batik dye) to the boil in a decilitre (sixth of a pint) of water in an old pan. Hold the flowers or grasses in the gently boiling water for a few minutes, swirling them about. Then let them drain and put them on newspaper to dry. Hang them up in a dry place for a little while until they are thoroughly dry. Butcher's broom (*ruscus*) can be dyed brown or dark green in this way. Spraying the dried flowers or grasses and grains is quicker but also more expensive, partly because much of the paint is wasted. If these techniques have made the colours of the arrangement too bright, this can sometimes be remedied by putting the flowers in bright sunshine for a few days. The colours will fade, and as a bonus the arrangement takes on a somewhat 'antique' appearance.

SOME PRACTICAL TIPS WHEN USING DRIED MATERIALS

Some kinds of dried flowers and leaves have stems that are brittle or too short, so they need to be reinforced or lengthened using rose wire or steel wire. This can be obtained in various thicknesses from florists and garden

centres. Fig. 4 shows how to set about reinforcing or strengthening stems in this way.

Alternatively, the stem can be wrapped with floral tape to hide the steel wire, starting immediately below the flower (fig. 5). Instead of a single bloom a spray of flowers can be used, into which attractive gradations of colour can be worked. It is easy to form a spray like this by twisting the stems of a number of flowers around each other (fig. 4). If wire has been used to strengthen the stems beforehand, the spray can now be bent into any desired shape. Sprays of flowers can be made from hydrangeas, xeranthemum, millet, pieces of Iceland moss (fig. 4) and so on.

You can also make a branch with flowers on it in this way. Starting at the top, the topmost flower is placed on a main stem, which is made from a long piece of 1 mm steel wire. The side flowers are fixed to this main stem using floral tape (fig. 5).

For making arrangements using dried flowers you have a wide choice of containers such as baskets, dishes, pots, pans, hats and vases because the receptacles do not need to be watertight. The nicest things are often to be found on rubbish heaps, at jumble sales, or in the cellar or attic. The most important thing is that the container's colour and shape should match both the flower piece that is to be composed and the surroundings in which it will be placed.

Once a container has been chosen, a styrofoam or oasis base should be placed in it. The foam can easily be cut to the desired shape using a bread knife (fig. 6a). Ensure that the foam is somewhat larger than the opening, because you must be able to position it so that it fits tightly. Another option is to secure a flower pricker on the bottom of a bowl or pot using, say, double-sided fixer or self-hardening clay on to which the foam is then pushed (fig. 6b). If the bowl or pot is rather light relative to the arrangement it is to hold, it can be weighted down

4 *Lengthening or strengthening flower stems*

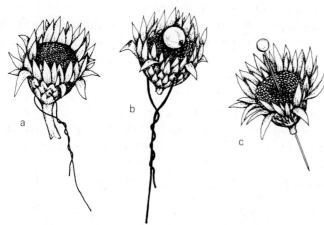

a. *insert thin rose wire through the base of the flower head*
b. *a bead can lend an attractive touch*
c. *secure small flowers without stems to a base using map pins*

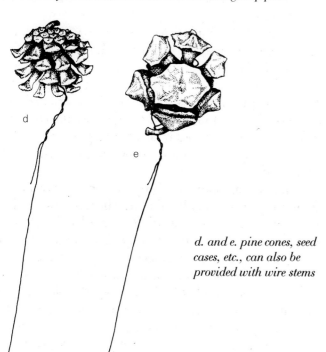

d. *and e. pine cones, seed cases, etc., can also be provided with wire stems*

by placing a plastic bag of silver sand at the bottom and inserting pieces of gravel down the sides (fig. 6c). However, if the container is to be a flat basket or a rush base, the foam cannot be held in this way. Instead, it must be secured to the background using a length of wire. A strip of net, thin material or plastic must then be placed under the wire (see fig. 13), otherwise when you pull the wire tight it will cut through the foam like a knife. Use pincers to twist together the lengths of wire underneath the basket or mat and cut off the superfluous bits.

f. *making a cluster*

g. *making a spray of Iceland moss or reindeer moss*

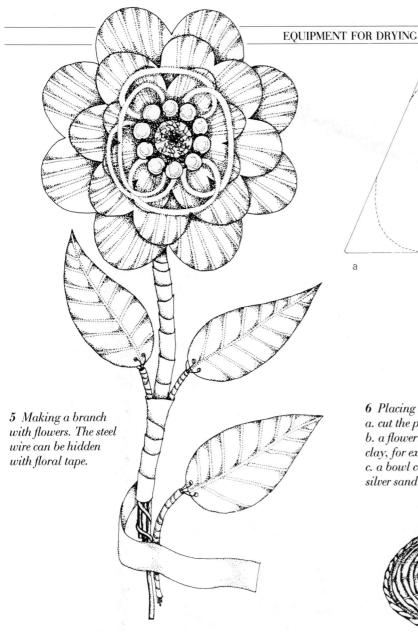

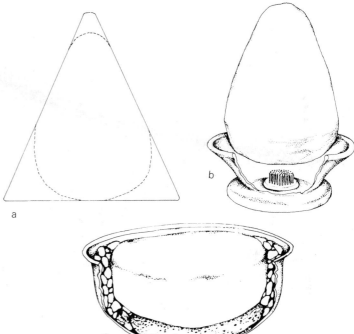

5 *Making a branch with flowers. The steel wire can be hidden with floral tape.*

6 *Placing a piece of foam into a pot or bowl*
a. cut the piece of foam to the desired shape with a bread knife
b. a flower pricker is stuck down in the bottom (using self-hardening clay, for example), and the piece of foam pushed down onto it.
c. a bowl can be weighted down by placing a plastic bag full of silver sand in the bottom, with pieces of gravel around the foam.

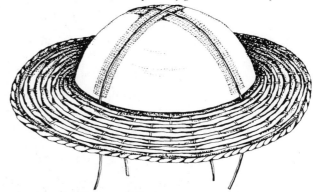

Opposite *A rustic still-life with hints of Van Gogh: dried sunflowers intermingle with yellow and brown tansies. The autumnal look is emphasized by the use of blades of grass, lonas and the receptacles of yellow cornflowers. On the table to the right is a dried artichoke.*

7 *Alternatively the piece of foam can be fixed to a flat base using wire (under which are strips of net etc.)*

3 WILD FLOWERS

Wild flowers must be picked with care, as some are very rare and are protected by law. You must always check on the laws governing the protection of wild flowers in the country that you are in before picking any of them. If you do gather plants in the fields or along the roadside, always do so with consideration. Never uproot a plant completely, and never take anything, flowers or seeds, that will not be used.

It is a much better idea to start your own wild flower garden, which can be done in a corner of the garden, in tubs on a terrace, or even on a balcony.

Below a number of species are described that are attractive and can even be grown on a balcony.

Bladder campion (silene vulgaris)
During flowering the calyx is flat, but later it forms bladders. These dry of their own accord and then look like little white or pink bells.

Catananche or cupid's dart
These are mostly seen as azure flowers, but when they have finished blooming a silver-white button appears. Very appropriate in small items or in white compositions. Catananche is not protected.

Chicory (cichorium intybus)
A plant whose flowers have light blue corollas. It branches irregularly so that when the flowers are over, the stems are interesting, with their very short stubby seed scales which dry naturally. Chicory is found by the roadside or field margins and waste ground. The plant is also cultivated. Beautiful in rust, brown and beige compositions.

Common evening primrose (oenothera biennis)
Plants with large yellow flowers that open in the evening. The plant was once eaten; now people collect the lovely seed pods, which grow close together. These seed heads can be gilded and pushed into clay to make a ring round a candle. But they do need to be soaked beforehand or they will break when handled. A whole stick of seed heads gives a splendid aspect to a brown, red and gold arrangement. According to legend, the evening primrose was one of the magic plants with which wild animals could be tamed; its sap was mixed with wine and the animals given it to drink.

Common toadflax (linaria vulgaris)
The strong yellow toadflax is found widely on roadsides. The insects have to push the flower open and in doing so they come into contact with the anther and stigma, making the fertilization process something of a snack during a burglary. That delightful little plant eyebright belongs to the same family. Look out also for *linaria maroccana* which is a cultivated plant and has splendid colours.

Common valerian (valeriana officinalis)
A perennial which occurs in the wild. It forms pinkish, dense flower heads which need to be picked whilst they are still in bud. They open out more during drying, and look beautiful with lavender (*limonium*). *Callicarpa* too goes very well with the bright violet berries of valerian that form in the autumn.

Common valerian

Dock or sorrel (rumex)
Plume-shaped clusters which turn first green and later reddish-brown. From a distance sorrel sometimes makes a meadow or grass verge look completely red. Both colours are lovely in arrangements of wild material.

Flax (linum)
Flax can be found here and there in the fields, though not by the roadside as such. It is used to make linen. Flax has many small leaves on a long stem, in which are immensely strong fibres that are spun into thread. Flax has azure or white flowers and the seeds form little hard spheres that can be painted gold. Flax is also grown in gardens, with white or red flowers. These perennials can withstand hard winters. The stems are much thinner and the seeds smaller, very charming in small bunches. Lengths of rose wire can be used to tie them into small tufts. An even more delicate plant to use is the amianth that grows on duneland.

Grasses (gramineae)
The grasses are an extensive family which includes 700 species. An interesting one is *wood millet*, a tall grass found in damp woods and shady spots. It forms a plume with oviform ears, a smooth stem and broad leaves.

Cocksfoot

Sweet vernal grass, bitter tasting and sweet-smelling gives freshly mown hay its fragrance. In damp spots, in meadows and roadsides one can find tussocks of *spear grass* with wide, decorative plumes. *Meadow-grass* is also a plumed grass, but *cocksfoot* forms denser, firmer tufts. *Meadow foxtail* is a green-beige species on a thin stem. A simple grass with long, sausage-shaped spikes is *timothy*. *Cotton-grass* occurs in swamps and wet bogs and has silky tassel fruits that resemble blobs of cotton wool.

Grains in wonderful shapes and colours can also be found on arable and meadowland, for example *maize, rye, wheat, couch-grass* or *twitch*, species of *barley*, the *wild oat* species and *rushes*. Rushes grow near and on marshes on damp sandy soils and heaths. They get their silky sheen from the tiny hairs that grow below each spike. Buds form in clumps below the top and make round balls of brown flowers. Arrangements made from materials like these cost nothing and do no harm to nature.

Hemlock (conium maculatum)

Very characteristic large white umbels and egg-shaped fruits. They can grow quite tall and are very poisonous. When they wither they smell of mice. The stems are bare, with red spots towards the bottom. The bear's breeches *(acanthus)* has an even larger umbel and very large leaves.

Lady's-mantle (alchemilla mollis)

This has yellow-green star-shaped flowers with no corolla. The leaves are positioned like capuchins around the stem – hence its common name, for a capuchin is a woman's cloak with a hood. The flowers create a lacy 'antique' effect. They are fragile and so must first be sprayed with water or stored in the cellar before use. They go well with gypsophila and *limonium*.

Mistletoe (viscum album)

This is a parasite with leathery olive-green leaves. Around Christmas-time poisonous white berries appear, which nevertheless are eaten by some thrushes. The seeds are then spread via the birds' sticky droppings. If they find their way into cracks in apple or pear trees they establish themselves parasitically. Thick dark clumps of mistletoe develop, creating a very strange effect, especially in winter, which is why popular superstition used to hold that the devil lived in it. For that reason, in Holland it has the alternative name of 'devil's nest'. It will be no surprise to learn that apart from its diabolical aspects mistletoe is also thought to possess magical powers. In Switzerland it was thought to indicate that there was treasure under the tree in which it was growing, while in England it brings luck to whoever walks under it.

Mullein (verbascum)

This plant has sulphur-yellow flowers and long, pointed leaves. The seeds adorn the roadside like candlesticks.

Large-flowered mullein is rather rare and has large flowers. In France shepherds used to gather its torches when the flock was moved to the high meadows of the Massif Central or the Alps for the summer months. In these lonely areas the torches, dipped in molten resin, served as natural lamps.

Opposite Variations on the poppy. Although the poppy becomes rather stiff when removed from its natural habitat, it can still be used to great effect in loose arrangements like this one without too much extra effort. Here the heads of the poppies have been given prominence and form an attractive pattern which has been enlivened by the addition of yellow ageratum, white edelweiss, a few flax fibres, a little sprig of green marjoram, radish seed, and a few asphodels and thistles. On the right is a lobelia killed by frost, and an ear of millet.

Old man's beard (clematis vitalba)

Old man's beard winds its way metres high through hedges and bushes. It can easily reach 18 m (60 ft). The flowers grow in pure white clusters which later form white, woolly blobs and then produce lovely material for use in filling garlands. The fluffy fruits need cutting off when they are feather-shaped and have not yet fallen off. The best thing to do then is to keep them in place by lightly going over them with hair spray. They are very decorative, and if a touch of blue paint is applied and the whole inserted into a bottle, a radiant summer sky effect is created. Old man's beard propagates easily, and the seeds are so light that they are spread by the wind.

green berries which turn bright red in autumn. Picked in their different seasons and allowed to dry in glycerine, the berries are excellent when used in combination with small roses.

St John's wort (hypericum perforatum)

A commonly occurring yellow flower with tiny holes in its leaves. In fact these are not really holes but small oil glands. The name is no doubt connected with St John having been burnt to death in boiling oil. The herb grows on dry ground along roadsides and among grass. After flowering, its sturdy brown seeds are lovely as background in an arrangement.

Old man's beard

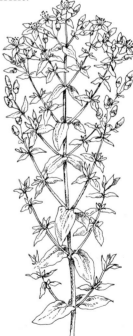

St John's wort

Rowan or mountain ash (sorbus aucuparia)

A shrub which makes its home in open, deciduous and coniferous woods where there is abundant bird life. The flowers bloom in umbels and in summer they give small

Scented mayweed (matricaria chamomilla)

There are two species in the fields. They have white pendant ribbon flowers, and yellow tubelets form the heart on a receptacle with a very characteristic fragrance.

There is also a scentless mayweed. When they have finished flowering the receptacles are well worth gathering. Although this species is not the 'true' chamomile, it is the one usually sold as chamomile tea.

Shepherd's purse (capsella bursapastoris)

This lies flat on the ground like a little sun rose. It has small white flowers and is delightful in a small display.

Soapwort (saponaria)

A strong plant with long stems that bend easily. Oblong leaves. The pink, fragrant flowers grow on branched inflorescences. A kind of soapy lather is produced when the flowers are dried and then rubbed between the hands with water. For this reason it was used in the past for doing the washing in remote settlements, where it was sought along the rivers. Nature supplied this alternative soap free of charge. Soapwort thrives by water. It is now grown also as a garden plant, particularly in wild gardens or rough corners, as it can withstand very cold weather. In autumn the tufts of seeds can be harvested. They resemble the seeds of the lilac and look splendid when sprayed gold.

Tansy (tanacetum vulgare or chrysanthemum vulgare)

This is a common plant which grows on grass verges and amongst low shrubs. The yellow umbels are delightful and must be gathered when their colour is plain to see. They then feel solid and hard. When flowering is over the umbels are dark brown, and look very decorative with white and gold materials. If appropriate a little gold paint can also be applied, so long as this is done in such a way that the original plant remains recognizable. Traditionally tansy and wormwood were used as charms against thunder, to appease the evil gods of the air. A dried bunch was burnt in the fireplace and the smoke then spread a protective layer over the house.

Weld (reseda luteola)

Oblong, fragrant spikes with small yellowish-green flowers. The seeds resemble those of shepherd's purse. The fruits are larger and grow right next to the stem. Also occurs in cultivated form (reseda odorata).

Wild carrot (daucus carota)

The white flowers grow in umbels and once they have flowered they close up like inverted umbrellas. They can also be used if they have turned brown. The flower resembles cow parsley (anthriscus sylvestris), which, however, blooms earlier in the spring. The flower is like a lace collar with green edging. The seed pods of both kinds can also be dried in a press. They produce lacy effects, as do also the flowers of goutweed, salad burnet and jack by the hedge (also known as hedge garlic).

Wild carrot

Yarrow (achillea millefolium)
This is a white flower with feathery leaves. It grows plentifully on verges and has a rather sharp fragrance. The white, sometimes pinkish flower heads are easy to dry when tied in bunches. In late autumn the heads are brown and combine beautifully with a touch of gold on them. Seed heads that have grown crooked produce lovely effects and can be used with the wild yellow milfoil, paper or silk roses and everlasting flowers in round compositions. The flowers can be pressed up firmly against each other to form a sphere.

When you have learnt to recognize the sort of plants that will be useful, you can add some new and interesting plant species to your existing supply from abroad, if you are holidaying there. For example, the chalky Causses, the stony plateaus of central France, are a good area for finding interesting subjects to go into dried arrangements:

Asphodel (asphodelus cerasifer)
This plant has branches with globes on, and also grows on the plateau. Its long stems with white flowers often grow to a height of 1 m (3 ft). Sheep must not eat it, so the plants are able to develop unhindered, to the joy of

Opposite Memories of autumn: a round arrangement of rust brown and terracotta red flowers which looks as though it has been burned by the sun and the hot summer wind. The basis of the arrangement is brown-painted ruscus with its sometimes fan-like effect. In between is anaphalis, painted reddish brown; a few tansies and small thistles, some sprigs of reindeer moss, pink plumes of knotgrass, and a variety of millet. The bowl of flowers is made to look a little more stylish using bent twigs of rhus typhina pointing outwards in all directions from the bottom of the arrangement. In amongst all this natural beauty are a few beige and brown artificial flowers made of velvet and warm red bead leaves.

the flower-loving tourist. The seeds, which dry naturally, are like small wild cherries and they are an elegant constituent in an arrangement of plateau materials.

Butcher's-broom (ruscus aculeatus)
This decorative evergreen shrub grows in undergrowth. Ruscus has small, hard, pointed leaves, and smooth stems the colour of oak leaves. In the spring it produces

Butcher's-broom

pale, greenish-white shoots which are edible. These resemble asparagus and indeed the plant belongs to the same family. The branches grow in wide curves, separately along the stem. It somewhat resembles the box, but grows in a much more elegant way. The box is denser, with a brown, woody stem, the branches more rigid and the leaves round. The leaves of butcher's-broom are almost the same colour, but those of box often fade to rust or red. In winter it forms dense red berries which readily fall off.

Butcher's-broom is very widely used as a starting or filling material, and is easily obtainable in all colours; it is even obtainable bleached. Because there is such a wide choice, it is easy to choose the wrong type. Sometimes the plant is so dressed up that the original is lost sight of. Pink, white, mauve or blue foam is sprayed on them and the result no longer has much connection with nature. It is often convenient to cut a number of small branches the same size and, using wire, work them into neat bundles which can then play their part in an arrangement. Because it is supple and does not break easily, its use involves few risks and a round arrangement can be quickly prepared. If you want a lively arrangement, use secateurs to cut off larger branches which can easily be arranged into the desired shapes. Ordinary holly is not so suitable for this kind of work, for it is too stiff.

You do not need to travel hundreds of miles for butcher's-broom: it can be grown in the garden and used as required.

Carline thistle (carlina vulgaris)

A really pungently scented plant with a fearsome number of thorns. Straw-coloured, and not to be taken hold of unless you are wearing gloves.

Unusual plants are not confined to the plateau in the south. If one goes down to the rivers or into low-lying woods there are various kinds for the plant-lover to find, such as:

Acanthus-leaved carline thistle or chardouse, the queen of the plateau (carlina acanthifolia)

This has practically no stem and spreads itself on the ground with a very prickly rosette. In chalky soils grows only to a certain height. The yellow inner bracts of the flower head open and close depending on the humidity. The flower-heads themselves are golden yellow, 11–15 cm (4–6 in) in diameter. When they close up in damp weather they look like plump onions, hence the French name of 'chardon-baromètre'. They are often seen nailed to the doors or shutters of houses as decoration. They are commonly gathered for sale, but this is prohibited in the Cevennes National Park.

Stemless carline thistle (carlina acaulis)

Decorative thistles grow on the plateau in numerous variations. This one grows without a stem directly on the stony soil, forming a splendid rosette with a single white flower head. It also grows abundantly in the Alps.

4 FLOWERS FROM THE GARDEN

You can be a gardener without necessarily having a proper garden. A window ledge, balcony or even a roof can serve the purpose. True, something of this kind is the bare minimum, but the amount of work that needs to be put into it is proportionately small. If there is a patch of soil available the possibilities are legion. The list of flowers in this chapter is confined to the species needed for the arrangements in the book.

Because our summers are short, it makes sense to sow at the right times. Some plants are propagated in advance, and this can be done in a greenhouse, a cold frame, in a window box or on the balcony. The seeds are sown in garden soil at a depth which is about twice the thickness of the seeds – as old gardeners say, the seeds must be able to hear the church clock strike. Germinating seeds like moisture and the warmth of the sun. Cover them with very openly woven jute sacking kept damp using a water spray. Sea lavender *(limonium sinuatum)*, globe amaranth *(gomphrena globosa)*, tobacco, all species of helipterum and helichrysum, *xeranthemum*, and the yellow ageratum *(lonas)* can be propagated in this way. Sea lavender, for example, takes a considerable time to grow. It has gigantic rosettes and if it is sown too late you will harvest more rosettes than flowers. Although buds appear on the stems in autumn, they will not open because there is no longer any power in the declining sun.

Once the ground has lost its early chill, the following are sown direct into the soil: love-in-a-mist, gypsophila, poppies, a pleasing meadow mixture of cornflowers, ox-eye daisies, yarrow, corn-cockles, various kinds of delphiniums, snapdragons, daisies, and so forth. Sowing must be carried out very thinly, and plants with tap roots, such as the poppy, must be thinned out, for it is very difficult to plant them out. Seeds that take a long time to germinate should be sown in rows and the seed-bed marked out by means of fast-growing vegetables such as lettuce and radishes as all these plants show their presence by two light-green lobate leaves. It is then easy to see exactly where to expect the flowers. The lobate leaves are different from the final foliage; thus delphiniums and columbine start off with a lobate leaf and become delicately feathery in appearance. Of course, the bed must be kept thoroughly free of weeds. For the keen gardener, spring is the most exciting season, for it is then that the work needs to be done if one wants to have something to harvest in winter, as La Fontaine relates so tellingly in the fable of the ant and the cricket; the ant industriously fills up his storehouse for as long as there is something to tuck away there and the silly cricket wastes his time in singing and dancing.

When the flowers are ready to be harvested, gather your materials when the heat of the day is to some extent past, on a dry day with a light breeze – a traditional good clothes-drying day.

Below is a short list of rewarding garden plants whose flowers and/or seeds can be included in arrangements:

Ammobium
A spherical white flower with a yellow centre. They can be gathered as buds or as flowers. This is a perennial. The centres will turn brown if you pick them too late. Dry them in the dark, hanging them upside down as always in such circumstances.

Black-eyed Susan (rudbeckia laciniala)
These have strong yellow flowers. The greenish-brown spherical flower head can be dried. To do this, we strip off the yellow petals and hang them up in bunches. They can be used in all arrangements. This is a perennial plant.

Blazing star (liatris spicata)
A plant that flowers differently from other composites. It forms an upright purple spike that flowers from top to bottom. Usually there are still buds at the bottom when the top is in bloom. It provides a lovely purple colour in arrangements.

Butterfly bush (buddleia)
The shrub produces violet flowers which are very attractive to butterflies, hence the name. In the autumn the spikes fade to a lovely brown, at the same time becoming hard. Even in winter they retain their charm, and are ideally suitable for autumnal compositions.

Candytuft (iberis amara)
Blooms in hyacinth-like clusters. The seeds can be used for decorations. If the seed pods are still attached, they form little balls. A little later on these develop into silvery clusters and sow themselves for the next year.

Chinese lantern or Cape gooseberry (physalis alkelungi)
This too is a well-known old-fashioned flower. It grows on a root-stock, but the small, greenish-white flower does not amount to a great deal. In the autumn the orange lantern-shaped seed-cases appear, hanging from curved branches. In the centre of each one is an edible berry. The lanterns easily dent, but you can inflate them again so long as the air chamber is not torn. In late autumn and winter the mesophyll – the fleshy inner tissue of the leaf – decays, leaving the main and side veins behind in a lacy pattern. This can be used in a flower 'painting', as decoration around or over another flower.

The Inca plum, which was introduced into our gardens from Peru, strongly resembles the fruit of the Chinese lantern. Its fruits are pale green and a little rounder than the lanterns. Again there is an edible berry in the middle of each fruit, tasting a little like a gooseberry and delightful for jam-making or for use as a dessert. Because of its individual colour the Inca plum is lovely in arrangements.

Opposite A garden arrangement. In the foreground, from left to right, can be seen seed radish, poppy, leek, onion, wild carrot and oats. Next to them are immortelles bound together in a large bouquet. In the grape-basket on the left are pink xerantherum together with yellow tansy and above it honesty. Climbing up the rake, which is also made from natural materials (in this case French nettle-tree, a variety of ash), is the brilliant orange of the Chinese lantern plant. Seed radish, light green marjoram, yellow lonas, a withered obedient plant (physostegia virginiana) which looks like bell-heather, and seed tobacco hang beside the lantern plants. The garland around the head of the statue head is made from plaited broom and stonecrop, faded milfoil and lonas. Behind him is a bunch of seed capsules from an evening primrose. The basket in front of him offers a selection of various weeds, sweet gale or myrica and painted anaphalis. The small fruit-picker's basket is full of lavender and pink helipterum. The large bunch of yellow flowers on the right is a variety of wild catsfoot. In the blue watering can are white xerantherum and seed radish. The bird sitting on the nest of flowers is made of coconut fibres and on the very far right of the picture is a flowerpot of ruscus, or butcher's broom.

Dame's violet (hesperis)

As a cut flower dame's violet is pleasantly scented, with purple, white or violet flowers – they resemble those of lady's smock (cuckoo flower) – any of which can be used. However, flowers that have finished blooming are well worth having in your stock of dried flowers, to represent the countries around the Mediterranean Sea where it originated.

Fern-leaved yarrow (achillea filipendulina)

Tall, stately plants with small petals and flat clusters of golden-yellow flowers that feel dry to the touch. When the clusters are hard they can be hung up to dry. They have a strong, characteristic scent. A round composition can quickly be made by arranging the clusters closely against each other. The interstices can be filled with, say, tufts of lavender-coloured statice, love-in-a-mist or everlastings. The little yellow milfoil *(achillea tomentosa)* is also very suitable for filling holes in arrangements. In autumn the clusters turn brown. Applying a little gold paint gives them a festive look, and they can then play their part in Christmas creations. But when flowering is completely over they take on a lovely pale brown tint which gives a typically natural effect. Strip off the leaves before drying. Because they are a perennial they will give pleasure in the garden for a long time. White and yellow yarrow *(achillea millefolium)* can be found wild, along roadsides (see previous chapter).

Globe amaranth (gomphrena globosa)

A flower for drying which requires a lot of sun. The flowers are carmine, cream and pink, and greatly resemble pink clover. They are easy to grow if you do not want to buy them in the market or at the florist's. The small hard globes fade quickly, making it advisable to spray them with hair lacquer or a fixative. There is also a miniature kind which is suitable for making candle rings,

and for this purpose they need to be stuck onto a disc of thick cardboard (fig. 8).

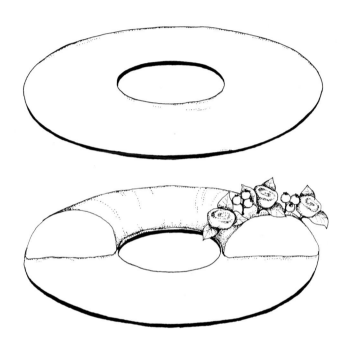

8 Making a candle ring on a cardboard disc, onto which the flowers are fixed in self-hardening clay

Globe artichoke (cynara)

The leaves are slightly prickly. The large heads have fleshy centres which taste delightful when boiled in salt water and dipped in vinaigrette. However, instead of serving them up topped with mushrooms, try enjoying them in a different way. The plants can be cut off as dense globes. There is so much moisture in their thick stems that they will open out as they dry. Consequently you do not need to place them in water, but simply dry them in a vase to produce violet flowers. When the flowers die, their hearts are ochre and the surrounding petals yellowish-brown, a very lovely combination. The dense globe can also be dried on a radiator, and each petal then opened out by hand in turn to produce a sort of green, dense, dry dahlia.

Various types of globe artichoke exist, such as the green of Laon, which produces violet flowers, and the *scobimus* with its blue flower. Completely different is the artichoke from Judea, which forms a creamy-white star, which comes from Israel.

Globe thistle (echinops ritro)
A tall plant with large, grey, dentate leaves. It flowers with dense blue heads that fall to pieces if picked too late. Dry them in bunches. The globe thistle goes beautifully with achillea and as a perennial will continue to be an adornment to your garden.

Golden rod (solidago)
This plant often performs the role of a golden-yellow background in the garden, and flowers in the autumn. It is so strong that it will grow through any rubbish. It also occurs in the wild and can be dried at various stages. Strip the leaves off and hang the spikes upside down. Even when winter is over they are attractive in an arrangement. By then they have become beige spikes, and shaking them leaves a little tail. Old books repeatedly claim that tea made from golden rod is good for sorrow in love!

Gypsophila
This is an old-fashioned plant, and there are annual and perennial varieties. They flower with small white or pink flowers on widely branching stems. They are excellent for preparing light and airy arrangements, including spherical ones. There are also very suitable as background in a glass dome or as a base in a white and cream combination. Gather when the white is clearly visible, and dry them upside down in the dark or upright in a vase with some water in it. The white or pink blobs shrivel up but remain decorative, even in small flower pieces. If the stems should break, gather a few tufts together using a length of thin rose wire. Gypsophila imparts an air of old-fashioned distinction to an arrangement. A common English name for it is 'baby's breath'. Sprays of it are often included in bridal bouquets.

Hebe (hebe Armstrongii)
Another delicate white branch for drying that is found in heather gardens. It is half shrub and half perennial. A hard winter will kill it. The tiny flowers are at the top of the stems. The plant belongs to the genus *Veronica* as does the lovely speedwell.

Helipterum manglesii or rhodanthe manglesii
This is everlasting. The flowers are on gossamer stems and resemble daisies in fine silky-white and soft pink. The leaflet is wrapped around the stem. They are difficult to use in a dry state because the stems are very brittle. The best way is to loosen the bunches after drying and then immediately put them into suitable vases; they will arrange themselves. It is almost impossible to put this species into oasis or styrofoam, but they can be used to fill gaps in a composition. They will then retain their position between other, sturdier blooms.

There is an even more delicate variety, with small bell-shaped flowers which do not open so far. Then there is also the bright yellow *helipterum humboldtianum*. It forms composite spherical flowers and the plant is aromatic.

Helipterum roseum or acroclinium roseum
The leaflets are small and greyish-green. When the flower is open its centre is disc-shaped. It requires a sandy soil and full sun. Varieties range from splendid

deep pink, light pink with a dark centre to white. The stems break easily when you are gathering them; however, even broken flowers can be used (figs. 4a and 4c). In bud form they are very picturesque in round arrangements. Indeed, these could well be the most attractive small roses for this kind of display. They are hung up in the dark to dry, and will then open further. If they are picked too late, they turn a dingy brown or yellow and the petals fall off. This everlasting also likes water, as was demonstrated by the wet summer of 1978. When the sun finally appeared, we were able to pick really splendidly-coloured giant everlasting roses.

Honesty (lunaria)

This thrives in light shade, producing white, lilac, pink or bright violet blooms which are among the harbingers of spring. The plant's beauty is threefold. In summer when the 'pennies' form green-red seed-pods they are lovely if used in dried-flower 'paintings', in other words on a flat surface, perhaps with small hydrangeas, because of their fascinating colour variations.

In the autumn they form silvery ovals, consisting of two egg-shaped bracts and a central petal. The brown kidney-shaped seeds sit in between. They are ripe when the two bracts can be removed using thumb and forefinger, the silver central petal remaining on the stem. The plant is self-sowing and is a biennial. If the plants are left in the garden undisturbed, the wind blows the seed pods off, and a little field of silver results. After six weeks of snow and wind they change again, looking like modern sculptures made of wire. We gathered them and quickly sprayed them with blue car paint, creating a wonderful effect. On a flat surface the white 'pennies' are

Opposite A thoughtful-looking, brightly-coloured angel and a Victorian posy bowl with similarly bold colours.

a good way of representing a fish's scales or a cockerel's feathers, when combined with dried ferns.

It is an easy plant to grow. Sow in the open, but choose the position carefully so that the plants will flower in light shade.

Hydrangea

This is an old-fashioned flower in beautiful colours ranging from purple to dark red and blue-green, its hues depending on the soil type. Hydrangeas are suitable as background; they cover oasis easily, and smaller flowers remain firmly held in them. There are two types of flower: the spherical ones and the long white funnel-shaped ones. The individual flowers also have splendid shapes so that one can spray a whole flower gold and place it on an old clock or cupboard in the company of tansy, also sprayed, or gilded yarrow that has finished blooming. Another variation is to place a gold-sprayed hydrangea on a flan tin, also sprayed gold, as the centre piece of a festive table. It is not difficult, and the flowers dry naturally.

Knotgrass (polygonum)

Pinkish-red flower spikes. Likes a lot of sun and warmth. The leaves are dark green and are commonly seen in borders. In the winter they seem to be dead, but they revive with the coming of spring. They can be dried hanging up in bunches, or in a press if you wish to use them in flower paintings.

Larkspur (delphinium)

There are two species: the annual, which is self-sowing; and the perennial, which has larger flowers and fine colours – lovely tints of dark blue, light blue, mauve and strawberry. They must be picked before they are at the peak of flowering, or the bells will fall off. Store them in small bunches in a dark place. They also dry well in a tin of silica gel or in glycerine. They can be used in combination with pink or red roses.

Lavender (lavandula)

Lavender flowers with fragrant blue-violet spikes. The petals are small and curled. Farmers in southern Europe cultivate the plant for the perfume that can be distilled from it. Bee-keepers like to put their bees into lavender fields, for lavender honey has a delightfully perfumed taste. The plant likes a chalky soil. Wild lavender (*lavandula spica*) flowers later and the flowers on the spikes are not so dense, although just as scented. Dry it upside down in small bunches in the dark because it fades very markedly in the light. The loose seeds can be used to fill little cushions, dolls, and bags to make the linen cupboard fragrant. You only need to wave lavender about a bit to smell its heady perfume. In southern France there are numerous herb and lavender markets, for traditionally people have always adorned themselves with these fragrant and colourful flowers.

Lavender cotton (santolina chamaecyparissus)

Found in borders. Greyish-green dentate leaves with tall upright stems. The yellow flower heads are like little buttons. Lavender cotton flowers in July and August and is a perennial, occurring commonly in southern Europe. It resembles the buttonweed (*cotula*) and is easy to dry in the dark.

Love-in-a-mist (nigella damascena)

Tender blue flowers surrounded by lacy gossamer greenery. The fruits are beige but may also be maroon or violet if they have had a lot of sun. *Nigella* is easy to grow and sows itself. The seed pods are most decorative when cut and dried, and are particularly attractive when sprayed gold. In sprays of four or five stems it goes well amongst yarrow, *sedum* and *lonas*.

Love-lies-bleeding (amaranthus caudatus)

Has red flower tails that can be dried upside down in bunches. The variety *viridis* has pale green flowers. Small tufts can be secured on rose wire between gypsophila and reindeer moss in Christmas arrangements, garlands around a dish or a candle, and so on. They are very fragile and brittle, so wet them with a flower spray before picking them up to work with.

Malva crispa

A species of mallow with a decorative leaf which is a typical green colour. The large leaves are like those of kale and the whitish leaves are small. It can be eaten as a vegetable and used to decorate bowls of fruit or meat. The seeds are grouped around the stem and are greyish in colour.

Mountain everlasting or cat's-foot (antennaria dioica)

The flowers are small and white or pinkish-red. Grows on dry sandy and heath areas. It has been improved for the rock garden. Pick before it is in full bloom, otherwise the flowers fall off during drying.

Obedient plant (physostegia virginiana)

This is another perennial border plant producing lovely cut flowers. It blooms from July to September with violet-pink and white labiate spikes. The flower can be turned by hand and will remain in that positon for a while, hence its common name. If you want more plants, the roots can be divided. When flowering is over they are beautiful in small arrangements. The seed resembles branches of bell-heather.

Ornamental onion (allium)

Lacy spheres which can be harvested at various stages, just like leeks which are allowed to go to seed. When the weather is dull and dark they too take on a dark-grey colour and come to resemble a rolled-up hedgehog; when it is sunny they are lighter in colour. A bunch of leeks can be decorated in a most delightful way by inserting small real flowers, or 'flowers' that have been cut from old lace. These artificial flowers look more 'genuine' if a bead is placed in the middle of them, using rose wire (see fig. 4b). In this way an 'amourette' can be made from something quite ordinary.

Poppy (papaver)

Various species are distinguishable, from small to large. The wild corn poppy (*papaver rhoeas*) with its bright red flowers forms lovely seed pods which are used extensively in round arrangements wrapped round with gold wire (fig. 4a). The oriental poppy (*papaver orientale*) is much larger, rounder, and sometimes with vertical striations. The poppy is very easy to use in many ways. The giant sorts can be painted gold and mobiles made from them.

The fine, dark seed is sown quite early in the spring and the plants thinned out so that they are about 20 cm (8 in) apart. You can harvest fresh seed yourself. The poppy heads rattle like well-filled money boxes and there are natural openings under the stigmas through which the seeds come out.

Poppies are lovely when used in groups in brown and greenish compositions. A pyramid consisting only of poppies is also a very special sight.

Rhus typhina

Belonging to the cashew, or sumac, family, this plant is a true wanderer through the garden, appearing everywhere. In autumn it forms sturdy velvety dark-red spikes. The leaves are also worth having, for in the autumn they change colour from green to yellow and then red. The shrub will tolerate soot and dust and can even survive on industrial sites.

Shell flower or bells of Ireland (molucella laevis)

The stems are thickly covered with small bell-shaped leaves, the bells forming an attractive light green garland around the stalk. In warmer areas they are found in the open fields. They fade a little if dried in bunches, but remain lovely and green if dried in glycerine.

Siberian edelweiss (anaphalis yedoenis)

The daisy-like flowers are arranged in dense flower heads. The leaves are silver-grey and hairy. They must be picked before they are fully open and then dried in the dark. This results in a soft white colour and dense tufts. If they are allowed to continue flowering, they turn cream and become like open daisies. *Anaphalis* is frequently dyed in pastel tints and is a favourite for dried arrangements.

Sneezewort (helenium)

A strong, old-fashioned border plant with reflexed ribbon-like flowers forming high spherical brown or yellow seed heads. In dried form they are decorative in a wide range of combinations.

Statice or sea lavender (limonium)

There are a great many varieties of this, the ordinary kind being *statice sinuata*. They are much used in arrangements. The small funnel-shaped papery flowers are on tall stems that are not round but angular in cross-section. They flower in all pastel hues, purple, violet, mauve, yellow, pink, deep pink and white, and in southern Europe, where the air is so much bluer, one even sees them in a splendid azure. They are dyed to fiery reds, terracotta and so on, bright colours which quickly fade. Gathering and drying them is easy, but they fare badly in rain, for too much moisture makes them rot and turn a dingy brown. The whole plant is a fine, large rosette.

Also in this group are *limonium suworowii* which has spiked flowers. Their pink colour goes extremely well with gypsophila and green amaranthus. *Limonium tataricum* and *limonium latifolium* are perennials with innumerable small grey flowers. The plant branches richly, sometimes forming a lacy sphere. It is very suitable for use as background, but if a composition is in danger of becoming too stiff it can also be used to fill gaps and thereby create a more airy and playful effect. The branches spread out somewhat, but will last for years as a main or secondary filling material – and, just like people, they turn grey with age. These types are also called *limonium vulgare*.

In the Rhône delta along the Mediterranean there are great fields of lavender-blue, violet, white and lilac *limonium binervosum* in the autumn. The smooth stems have tiny buds on them. Because it grows by the sea it has the name 'Lavande de mer' (sea lavender). As it grows on salty clay, it cannot be cultivated in the garden.

Stonecrop (sedum)
A rock plant with small fleshy leaves. The flowers are small yellow or larger pinkish-white or dark-red umbels. In autumn they turn reddish-brown or chestnut and look very attractive in woody arrangements. After winter they bleach to an off-white. Like all umbels, stonecrop is easy to use in a composition. In addition the plant is easily satisfied, has an iron constitution and needs no attention.

Strawflower (helichrysum)
This is the easiest everlasting flower to use. An annual that used to be grown in country gardens side by side with hollyhocks, dahlias, hydrangeas, sweet williams, guelder roses, lupins and lilies, although it was not yet then fashionable to use the everlasting flower as the basis of a dried arrangement, and they were simply left to flower in summer as an out-of-doors decoration. They come in many colours: dark red, brown, pink, and sometimes even violet. They like plenty of moisture and manage to thrive even in rainy summers. The best way to dry them is upside down in small bunches in a dark, dry place. Sometimes they can be strung straight onto a length of wire after the leaves have been stripped off, but be sure to do this immediately after picking, or they will break. However, this method of working tends to make the arrangement rather stiff. They come in various sizes. The small compact varieties flower profusely with double blooms in ivory, pink and red. The bright yellow *helichrysum* is imported. The third variant is the 'bikini', which flowers for an enormously long time. *Helichrysum* can continue to be gathered until the frosts start, yet they are ready to pick early too, so that it is possible to take a few each day. They open further during drying, and time and again one is surprised by the richness of their palette of colours. Because of the water in their stems, they carry on blooming even after they have been picked. If the bud is too far open, seeds form and your attic or shed will be full of fluff. The receptacle becomes visible and the petals fall off.

Even if too many have been gathered to use in arrangements, there are ways to utilize the left-overs. A number of bunches can be tied together to make a large cluster. To do this, a stick is inserted into the first bunch

Opposite A basket of dried flowers which has been assembled using plants from each of the four seasons. The nosegay was begun in winter by picking thistles, which turn a pale colour because of the cold. In spring, daffodils were dried using silica gel. Summer brought yellow roses, both budding and flowering, which were placed in soap powder together with a few sunflowers. In early autumn tansies and green oats were harvested. A few pale yellow artificial flowers were used to fill the gaps. This is a composition which reflects some of the joyful vitality of nature and which shows the wide range of flowers available throughout the year.

and the other bunches tied around it using a long length of string. The whole is then hung upside down to give a floral atmosphere to the room (see fig. 9).

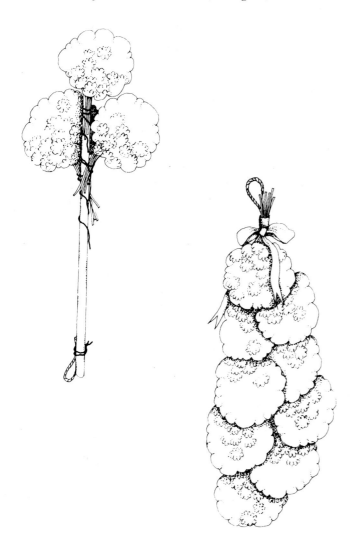

9 *A number of bunches of dried flowers are tied together round a stick (left) and hung upside down (right).*

Teasel (dipsacus fullonum)
A rough customer that can grow 2 m (6 ft) tall or more. Occurs commonly in the wild, producing large spherical flower heads with deep lilac flowers. The leaves grow in pairs along the stem, and where their bases join little pockets are formed which act as reservoirs for rainwater on dew. The birds have discovered that these are mini drinking troughs which still have water in them on dry days, giving rise to the French common name 'paradis des oiseaux'. Goldfinches are extremely keen on the seeds; in this way one facet of nature helps another. In earlier times wool was carded using these natural alternatives to steel brushes. Teasels are appropriate in coarse arrangements; they are self-sowing and dry naturally. Commercially, they are often obtainable dried.

Thorn-apple (datura stramonium)
Large rough shrubs with long white flowers. In the autumn they form large prickly seed cases which resemble the cases of horse chestnuts. These cases dry of their own accord and go well with holly and gold-painted poppies. A combination of these can be made into a decorative globe and hung from a lamp.

Autumn is the time to cut them or buy them, but some caution should be exercised as the seeds and other parts of the plant are extremely poisonous and can cause blindness. You can sow them yourself.

Vervain (verbena)
A plant which flowers in all pastel hues and which can also provide the basis for a herb tea or a delightful green liqueur. The umbels of the cultivated flowers can be dried in a press to give a circle of little flowers.

Woundwort (stachys)
Hairy herbs with strong leafed stems. The corolla is red or pale yellow. Occurs also on building sites.

Yellow ageratum (lonas)

This is an annual everlasting with groups of golden-yellow buds. Very suitable for plaiting into garlands, and decorative because of its warm golden-yellow colour. Gather when in full bloom. The flowers are harder than the violet ageratum and no extra drying agent is needed. *Lonas* is so woody that it will dry on its own in a dry place, but violet ageratum must be placed in silica gel. Both kinds are ideal in spherical arrangements.

Xeranthemum

In their earliest stage these are small, grass-like plants, from which a single stalk with a bud on it appears. Later they grow into large branched shrubs which can easily reach 1 m (3 ft). The flowers are on tall stems and are purple, pink and white.

The xeranthemum must be picked at the start of flowering, but it is very troublesome to gather. The bushes are full of buds and are a maze of stems. Because they do not all flower at once, it is not possible to pick a whole bunch quickly, as one does with immortelles. The greyish-green stalks of the plant are flexible and so can be plaited into lovely hearts and ovals or garlands. If you pick more than you can easily use at once the surplus must be kept in the refrigerator, for if the stems become too dry they will break when being plaited. If the nights turn too cold, the whole shrub can be cut down and allowed to dry so that there is still something to harvest even in the depths of winter.

Xeranthemum is a very precious flower that is fairly seldom available commercially, but in Greece it grows along the roadsides. It can, however, be grown by oneself. Dry this plant upside down in the dark. They are lovely in groups amongst an arrangement made from green oat spikes. Bunches of ten stalks can be fastened together using thin wire and used in an arrangement to good effect.

BUYING FLOWERS FROM SHOPS

Even if one has a large garden there may not be enough time to work in it, for flowers demand attention, knowledge and dedication; but one always has the option of buying flowers from a professional supplier. Not only can all the flowers described above be bought commercially, so can a whole range of exotic items from all parts of the world. Nor need your purchases at the florist's be confined to flowers, as branches, seed heads and foliage can be found there too.

From South Africa, for example, comes the illustrious *helichrysum vestitum* (Cape white or South African marguerite). Its stem branches at the top to give a whole cluster of flowers, up to eight, growing close up against each other, and this plant is always easy to include in arrangements. The petals are silvery white with a disc-shaped heart, very decorative and beautiful when used

10 An old garlic string from the market makes an ideal base for a dried flower arrangement. Make it more rigid by using thick wire and then just insert the flowers.

with other tints of white or cream. The flowers close up, however, if they become damp. Other plants to be found in abundance may include immortelles (*helichrysum*), found in all sizes and colours, the yellow ageratum (*lonas*), and the pink globe amaranth (*gomphrena globosa*). You will no doubt come across *anaphalis* and its little sisters, either white or dyed. The smallest everlasting flower is the glixia (see fig. 11b). Somewhat larger is the *botao bolina*. Then there is the pink exuberance of *helipterum* in their variations such as *helipterum manglesii* (*rhodanthe*) and *helipterum roseum* (*acroclinium roseum*). You may also find statice (*limonium*) in all gradations of colour, the greyish-white wood material of *limonium latifolia*, and the long pink tails of *limonium suworowii*, *xeranthemum*, gypsophila, dried larkspur (*delphinium*) in pink, violet, white or cream, the cultivated and wild achilleas, which has yellow umbels which one can also bleach to white, *hebe Armstrongii* (of the *Veronica* family), a delicate white dried flower from the heather garden. There is love-lies-bleeding (*amaranthus caudatus*) in red and green.There are also contrasts between the bright orange Chinese lanterns (*physalis*) next to the *albiflora* with its white spherical umbels, the sugar bush (*protea*) and branches of millet (*sorghum*) and bottle-grass (*setaria*). The various poppies, the oriental poppy (*papaver orientale*) and the opium poppy (*papaver somniferum*), reindeer moss, love-in-a- mist (*nigella*), lady's mantle (*alchemilla*), the hydrangea, *eryngium*, the globe thistle (*echinops*), the *allium* species (leeks, onions and garlic which have gone to seed), cock's comb (*celosia*), buttonweed (*cotula*), the *santolina* family and many others are all attractive to the dried-flower arranger. Even dried roses (*rosa*) can be purchased in pink,

Opposite An unusual container for an outdoor arrangement.

crimson, white and yellow. The white rose with red edges (*laminuette*) and the red rose (*ilona*), the Pink Puff, the white Jack Frost, the baby roses Menuet and Dr Verhagen can also be bought fresh and then dried in sieved shell-lime, silica gel or washing powder. They do fade, and it is therefore best to place your arrangement in a fairly dark spot. Roses acquit themselves well in combinations with hydrangeas. Roses with statice and gypsophila also produce a quick and elegant nosegay. Before purchasing, however, it is a good idea to select an appropriate container so that the choice of materials can be thought out properly.

If all this still makes you hesitate, there is yet another option for the unsure beginner, which is to buy a ready-made arrangement to use as a starting point and to add to it. There are now shops which sell nothing but dried flowers, so an excellent way of 'cheating' or getting to know which shapes work well, is to buy a few bunches of different kinds of dried flowers and experiment with them.

Finally, another piece of practical advice. When preparing a dried-flower arrangement, the oasis into which the flowers are inserted must be covered with some kind of base material. The following are serviceable: hydrangeas, dried clumps of weeds, faded everlasting flowers, heather, butcher's-broom (*ruscus*) or reindeer moss. This reindeer moss grows in the barren north and is food for reindeer, hence its name. It is imported by air, pressed, from Iceland, Lapland or Greenland, and is used extensively by florists in Christmas and funeral arrangements. Wet it before use, or it will break. Small tufts can be held together using rose wire and then fixed into the oasis (see fig. 4g). Its colour harmonizes particularly well with yellow roses. To some extent reindeer moss resembles the greyish-green lichen that grows like a mould on trees (and can even kill them).

Apart from the fresh roses already mentioned, one can

11 Hand-made paper flowers can beautifully complement an arrangement of dried flowers. They can be made simply and quickly from a wide range of materials, from crepe paper to gold or silver foil. Even a paper coaster can be transformed into a delightful 'rose' (c). Here are just a few ideas for you to try out.

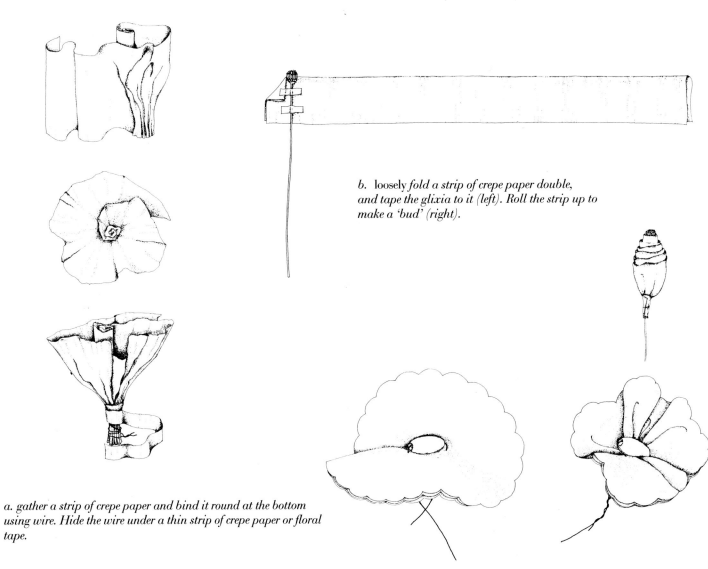

b. loosely *fold a strip of crepe paper double, and tape the glixia to it (left). Roll the strip up to make a 'bud' (right).*

a. *gather a strip of crepe paper and bind it round at the bottom using wire. Hide the wire under a thin strip of crepe paper or floral tape.*

c. *how to make a rose from a few paper coasters*

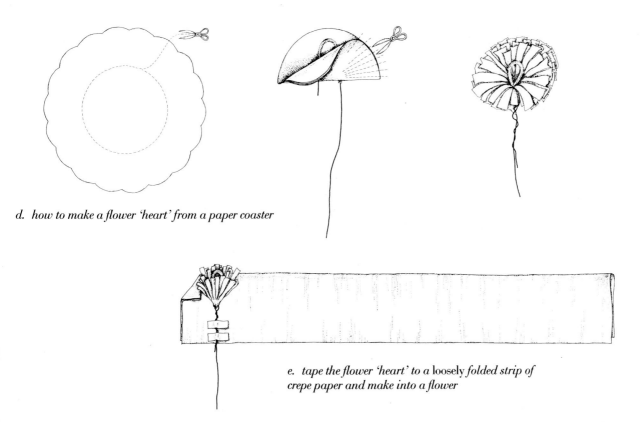

d. how to make a flower 'heart' from a paper coaster

e. tape the flower 'heart' to a loosely folded strip of crepe paper and make into a flower

of course also buy countless other kinds of flowers from the florist or flower-stall for home drying. The first ones that come to mind are gerberas, ox-eye daisies – in the centres of which a golden sheen appears on drying – zinnias, gazanias, snapdragons, freesias, carnations. And never throw old arrangements away, for they form splendid backgrounds. Some freshly dried flowers can be added to produce expanding arrangements that grow ever taller.

Any dried flower arrangement can be enhanced with the addition of hand-made paper flowers. Fig. 11 illustrates how a number of flowers can be made simply and quickly.

There are still some people who will not have dried arrangements in the house because they regard them as dust traps. It is not so much the natural flowers that get dusty as the ones made out of paper or gold foil. There are various cleaning methods:

i)   Blow the flowers clean using a hair-dryer, which of course should not be directed right at them.

ii)   Blow them clean using the output end of a vacuum cleaner.

iii)   Dust them using a soft badger-hair brush kept for the purpose, or using a feather duster.

iv)   But by far the simplest way is just to blow on them yourself now and again.

5 COLOUR

The interplay of natural colours forms the basis of all dried arrangements and the fascination lies not only in the splendid shapes which the many kinds of plants form, but also in the rich gradations of colour that can add a whole new dimension to a living space. Any biology book will tell you that the colours in the plant and animal worlds have an important influence on patterns of behaviour, because colours can attract or repel. But there is much less discussion of the sensitivity of humans to colours, quite possibly because people are a little shy of believing in the concept. That is why many will smile on reading that Madame de Pousillac, one of the ladies who maintained fashionable salons for artists and scholars in the eighteenth century, lamented that the tone of the conversation at her gatherings changed the moment she changed the colour of the décor from blue to crimson.

In fact human beings have always subconsciously taken nature as their master when working with colours. At sunset the daylight changes from a radiant white to yellow, orange and red. The beauty of the sky as the light fades at the end of the day is ever fresh, unlike the ominous darkness on the approach of a spring shower or an autumn storm. The dull grey of the clouds is quite different from the warm evening light as it changes imperceptibly to a cool dark blue. Warm colours are popular in the home because they give a feeling of well-being, and according to the wise Goethe they make one cheerful. Yellow, orange and bright red literally have a warming effect, and how delightful are autumn arrangements in these tints, capturing as they do the remnants of summer's warmth. Blue, on the other hand, is cool; not only does it imply something of darkness, it also creates a certain remoteness. Blue is the colour of distance: just as the sky above is blue, so is the horizon, veiled in a blue haze even on a clear day. Warm colours appeal to the eye and are restful. The colours of the rainbow range from warm to cool and are centred around green, which links both effects and creates a balance, just as in nature green, which is the dominant colour, supports the harmony of nature.

In order to exploit the richness of natural colours, it is necesary to know a little about colour relationships; not only relationships within the arrangements themselves but also with their surroundings. When making an arrangement you should think about where it will be placed; or – even better – if we have sufficient materials, we should compose it in position. Just as a painter examines his canvas now and again by stepping back a few paces, so you must look at the display in relation to

Opposite An unpretentious arrangement which gathers together many different flowers from an autumnal garden. A mixture of bright and faded colours complement each other beautifully and are arranged in a loose, flowing way which matches the flowing grace of the porcelain vase.

the whole room to make an unprejudiced assessment of the effect you have created.

If the harmony of the colours leaves a little to be desired, the overall impression will be gaudy; but this lack of balance is not necessarily unpleasant. On festive occasions colours should be bright. A brightly-coloured flower composition can distract attention from otherwise dull surroundings. However, if the colours chosen are too harsh, too strident, too obtrusive, the whole will take on an aggressive character and will seem in bad taste.

6 VICTORIAN NOSEGAYS

Although dried flower arrangements can look good in almost any surroundings, for many people they still spell nostalgia, the world of gleaming copper and pewter, of old pine dressers and chintz upholstery. The emphasis was on comfort and softly rounded edges, and this was reflected in the round designs of Victorian 'tussie mussies', posies and other arrangements. These circular displays can still create a warm comfortable feeling, especially on a cold winter's day when some pinks and golds will complement the light from a glowing log fire.

The photograph on page 57 shows a particularly lovely example of a Victorian posy bowl. The arrangement is a combination of brown and white, but don't let this put you off it: there is a great deal of beauty and subtlety in it. We picked tansies in late summer: these were in two colours, a slightly muddy yellow and a brown where autumn had started to take its toll already. Between these are Siberian edelweiss (*anaphalis margaritacae*) and different sizes of white catsear (*antennaria dioica*). The cones of the larch tree (*larix*) are dipped in gold paint. Buds made of white crêpe paper are attached to pieces of wire and at the centre is *glixia*, the smallest of the immortelles. The larger white flowers are bought ones, made of balsa-wood and feeling like paper flowers. The white side panels are filled with honesty (*lunaria*). A few corn poppy heads (on the right) have had gold paper wound round them (see fig. 14), whilst above them, some gold-painted cloves can just be seen.

Making a round Victorian-style nosegay arrangement
Materials:
butcher's broom (*ruscus*) sprayed green and cut into smaller pieces using secateurs
small pine or larch cones
grey-white *limonium*
some fluffy alder balls
cloves
poppy heads small and large
(All the above can be sprayed gold.)
thistles, for instance the woolly alpine thistle (*cirsium*)
small and large yellow and red plastic balls (on sale in stores at Christmas for decoration)
paper or fabric roses, which can also be made from paper coasters
floral wire (green) in various thicknesses
gold paint, gold wire or gold spiral

All these materials should be placed within reach so that you do not have to keep putting everything down whilst you are working.

Start by choosing the top of the arrangement (fig. 12). This could be a branch of *ruscus* with a longer stem (or lengthened using wire, fig. 13), a thick poppy head which has been sprayed gold, or a red plastic ball on a wire. Stems of *ruscus* are then wound around this. Again winding them round, fasten some *limonium* between, now a cluster of three small plastic balls, then a gilded pine cone amongst them, a beech nut alternating with a

12 Making a Victorian-style round nosegay in Christmas colours

a. start with a small rose, a stem of ruscus or something similar, around which a second stem or flower is wound

c. finish off the arrangement by hiding the steel wire under floral wire or crepe paper and placing a paper doyley around the stem

thorn-apple fruit or a small silver thistle. Wind the *ruscus* around in such a way that a kind of tree is created, paying attention to the kind of bowl or vase in which the work is to be placed. The wider the items are wrapped at the top, the broader the arrangement will become at the bottom. Paper roses in red, pink or white can also give extra colour when the tree is being filled out. *Ruscus* is generally very flexible. If it should be too stiff, it must be left outside or in a damp cellar overnight. During

b. wind more stems and flowers around it in turn

Opposite *A good luck bouquet for newly-weds. The sides of the arrangement are made of the fragile honesty, or Lunaria.*

13 *A cluster of* ruscus *is lengthened with wire*

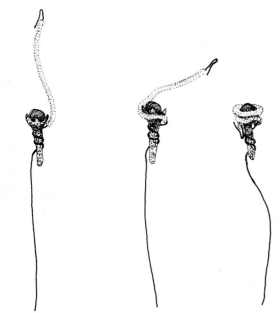

14 *A length of gold spiral is pushed onto a steel wire and wrapped around the clove or poppy head.*

preparation of the piece you must check continually, using your hand, that the whole arrangement is evenly round. Once the flower elements are satisfactory, the stems or wires should be cut off to the same length and tied together using string, elastic, wire, nylon or adhesive tape. If the arrangement is not to go in a vase but, for example, is to be hung on top of a lampshade, or simply placed somewhere on its own, the behind-the-scenes work on the stalks and wires must be hidden using green adhesive tape. A doyley cut from gold foil or a gold-sprayed flan dish is placed underneath (fig. 12c).

Not all these elements need be included in a single arrangement at the same time; they can be spread over different arrangements. If a cluster of *ruscus* is sticking out too far, it can simply be clipped off using scissors. After a little practice, an evergreen arrangement like this takes very little time and makes an enjoyable present which anyone would be happy to receive.

Try a variation on the Victorian Christmas colours, whilst still keeping to the round shape. The red-green combination looks lovely when supplemented with pink-violet, using all kinds of species of pink-violet and blue-yellow-white tufts.

Opposite *Making a Victorian arrangement.*

7   COMPOSITION

When you have mastered the art of nosegay-making, you can try other arrangements and shapes. First of all you need to draw a plan which takes into account the dried flower materials that are available.

If the container to be used is a basket that is to stand in the centre of the room so that it will be seen from all sides, the flowers must also be such that something of interest is visible from every angle. But if the basket is to go into a corner, then special attention must be paid to the face. You also need to decide whether the whole structure is to be tight and enclosed or open and airy, and also to be satisfied that you have the right flowers at your disposal (figs. 17, 18 and 19).

The illustration on page 63 shows some examples of how to work using baskets, pots, or woven mats. In the right foreground is a classical basket, not yet filled, with a block of oasis in it. The block must of course be fixed down firmly, e.g., by securing it with wire as here. As further reinforcement, a few good-sized stones can be pressed between the side of the basket and the oasis to give the basket more stability. The container can also be weighted down by placing in it plastic bags filled with silver sand. You must always be careful to see that the piece is not top-heavy. The wire used must be flexible or it will cut through the oasis; for that reason place a strip of net under the wire.

An oasis can easily be cut into any desired shape using a knife, the imagination can be given free rein. Hence on

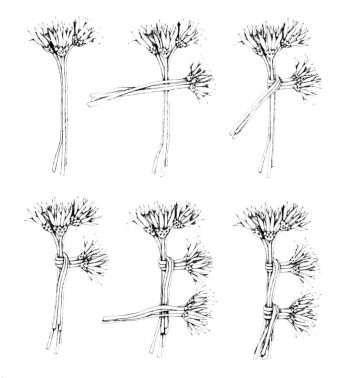

15 *Plaiting flowers*

Opposite *This close-up shows how dried flowers and artificial flowers can be arranged to great effect. Cream-coloured silk roses are combined with Cape white and edelweiss. A thin balsa-wood rose contrasts with the finer white colour of* hebe Armstrongii.

the left there are two heart shapes. The one nearest the front is already finished. Before starting it – and this is something one must always think of in the case of pieces that are later to be hung up – a coarse network is made around it using wire, with a loop. Then the outline is marked out using plaited everlasting flowers (*xeranthemum*). Plaiting is a skill that most people learnt as children and is shown in fig. 15. To get the right shape during this preparatory work, plaiting is carried out

along strong wire and then the whole secured at a few points to the styrofoam using pieces of rose wire. Gypsophila has been used to hide the background, and the heart has been filled with violet anaphalis and other bud-shaped everlasting flowers, such as glixia. An additional decoration an old gold tassel hangs at the point of the heart.

Behind the hearts is an old sugar bowl whose lid has long gone. The oasis is pressed firmly into this and then cut to the required height using a knife. Keep the cut-off pieces, which can be used as filling material. Candleholders do not need to be bought as such; the other one in the picture was home-made from the knob of a wooden curtain rod, filed down underneath so that it will sit firmly. A circle of styrofoam is supported by a decorative plate from the heating pipes – for clarity it is shown next to it in the picture – and is then covered with a base of reindeer moss (fig. 16). Then small flowers are inserted, as can be seen in the sugar bowl; these may be reinforced on wires. It takes a little work, but the result is worth the effort and if the candle does not burn down too far it is an inexpensive Christmas decoration. Behind the basket in the foreground are two round mats with a hemisphere of styrofoam (fig. 7), on the left the first stage and on the right the final result. There are two aspects that need attention when working with the flowers needed – and there are quite a few – to cover the surface. The round shape must be reproduced in the final result, which means that each element must be inserted firmly, yet not too deeply, into the hemisphere, so that there are no dips or hills in the flower surface. At the same time the colours need to be tastefully distributed. In this case darker colours have been chosen for the sides, becoming lighter towards the middle. Keep turning the mat

candle

oasis

covering-plate from central heating pipe

plasticine

knob of a wooden curtain rod

file down end

16 A candleholder you can make yourself

Opposite *Bases for flower arrangements and how they are built up.*

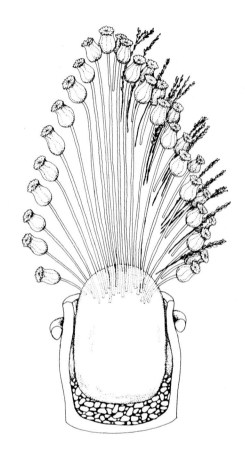

17 Plan for a flower piece. The flowers are inserted into oasis in the following order:

1. *yellow and brown tansy*
2. *lonas or yellow ageratum*
3. *yellow milfoil*
4. *brown sunflowers*
5. *yellow cornflowers*
6. *small poppy heads*
7. *grases and plantains*
8. *golden rod*
9. *pine cone*
10. *sea lavender*

18 Plan for a flower piece. Basic shapes and the end results obtained

Opposite *A tall arrangement of poppies. The stiffness of the poppies makes them ideally suited to making geometrical shapes, provided you are not too sparing with your materials. In this case a cone made of styrofoam has been used as the base for the arrangement. Once it has been filled with flowers it looks rather heavy and ponderous. The effect is lightened by using slender, wavy stems of grass in suitable colours so that in the finished arrangement there is no feeling of stiffness at all.*

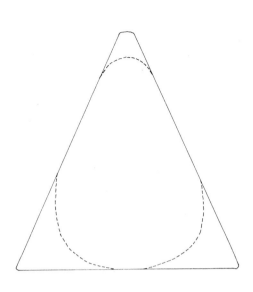

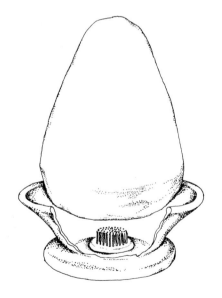

19 *Plan for a flower piece. The flowers are inserted into the oasis in the following order:*

1. *golden yellow and brown tansy*
2. *roses made from balsa wood*
3. *paper roses*
4. *paper rosebuds*
5. *anaphalis*
6. *rose heads wired to form a 'necklace'*
7. *poppy heads*
8. *pine cones*

round whilst you are working on it to check the shape, and walk round it a few times to examine the colour gradations in different lights.

Finally, at the back there are two oval mats. On the first, the outline has already been defined using plaited everlasting flowers. The first layer consists of *statice*, gypsophila and grey-white *limonium*. The whole arrangement has been made so that it can either lie horizontally or be hung up.

In the foreground there is a special badger-hair brush which is very useful for dusting dried arrangements. In the basket next to it there is a branch of dried *ruscus* in the styrofoam and the centre of a yellow cornflower that has finished flowering. The former points to the right, the latter more to the left. Each element has its own direction of growth, and as far as possible it is recommended that you keep the natural direction.

This is particularly important when preparing sparser arrangements which follow the characteristic lines of the plants.

Bead leaves are made as follows: on a length of rose wire string several beads, of a colour that matches the flowers. Now bend the wire round, winding the end around the longer part of the wire which is to be the stem. This completes the oval. If you want to make a double leaf, next take a shorter length of wire, which will then take fewer beads (fig. 20b). Close up this second leaf and place it with the first. Then fix the tail of the second leaf to the first stem. Now wind gold thread, or unravelled gold thread, in a criss-cross pattern around it, the beginning and end being tucked away amongst the steel wires. Of course, you can also further develop this leaf by applying a gold vein of thicker gold around it, wrapping the finer network around it. Then you can construct a flower shape from four bead leaves, and the centre of the flower is made from a number of gold beads or gold or silver wire. These artificial flowers use mainly

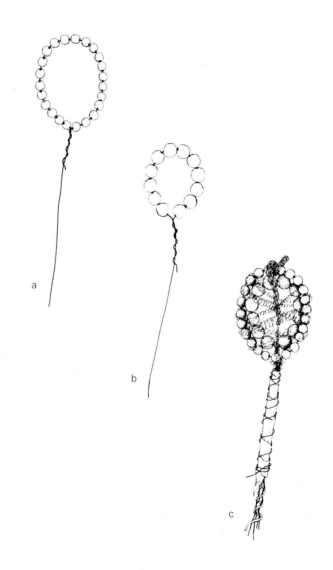

20 Making bead 'leaves'
a. the outer leaf
b. the inner leaf
c. wind gold thread in a criss-cross pattern around the two leaves

67

glass beads which are good and round, and match each other. Glass gives a special sheen, and reflects the light of its surroundings. Wooden beads are too dull. Using mother-of-pearl beads will give an even smarter effect, as they display all the colours of the rainbow. It may be difficult for some people to obtain these beads, but you may find them on an old necklace bought perhaps at a jumble sale.

The bead leaves that you have made must never become too strident. It is extremely ugly to have two bright colours in one leaf; on the other hand, it is lovely to have two closely-related colours such as white and cream, or two tints of blue or grey. Little garlands of dried flowers or seeds around a mirror or photograph can also be enlivened using beads. Gold thread can be bought in handicraft or haberdashery shops, where all kinds of tape, brushes, velvet, spangles and sequins, in short everything you are likely to need in this area, can be obtained. Silk, velvet and golden roses or other artificial roses can also be found there.

8 FESTIVE DECORATION

Important events in people's lives are nowadays recorded by means of photographs, which are quite likely to be taken by a hired photographer. In former times, unless one could afford a painter one had to make do with mementoes: the wedding dress, the bouquet, the shoes and presents all helped to keep the memory alive. Even today, when such occasions are not only captured by photographs, but also by the video camera, it is still a wonderful idea to preserve the wedding bouquet by drying.

Dried flower arrangements make attractive table decorations for festive occasions, Christmas for example. Such occasions provide a wonderful opportunity for incorporating homemade flowers into the design. The illustrations on the next few pages will give you some ideas for making flowers using gold foil and beads, and the photograph on page 73 shows what the finished effects can be.

The compositions previously described were based on a cone shape but in similar fashion one can make arrangements which are spherical or hemispherical.

To make the conical arrangement in the centre of the photograph on page 73, take a knife and cut a piece of styrofoam into half a cone lengthwise, so that its back is flat. A piece of cardboard is cut to the same size and the half-cone fixed to this using wire, and at the same time making a loop to hang the arrangement up by. Everything must be sufficiently sturdy, which is why no

21 *Making a tassel from gold foil*

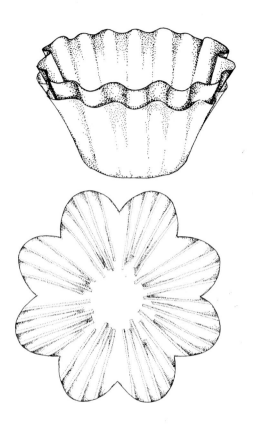

22 Making flowers from gold foil

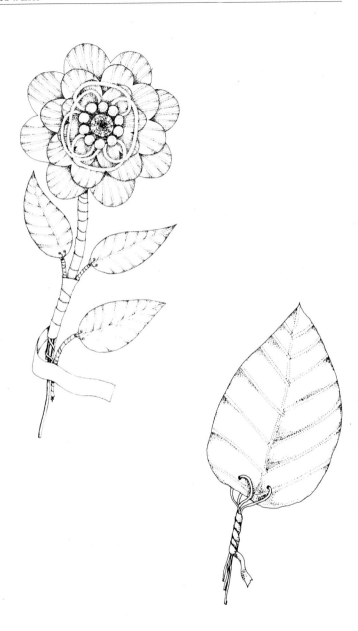

oasis is used, as it would tear too easily (fig. 25).

The *ruscus* is cut into small sprays and sprayed brown or gold beforehand. If the stems are not strong, reinforce them with wire (fig. 13). At the top is a branch of *ruscus* which waves beautifully, but an attractive hatpin or a tassel cut from gold foil can form the top. Now the cone is filled, a spray of brown, a small rose, santolinas wound with gold, poppy heads or cloves also wound with gold, gold-sprayed flax heads in tufts supported on wire, a thistle (fig. 26). Do not use vivid colours. The openings

23 Making a flower branch

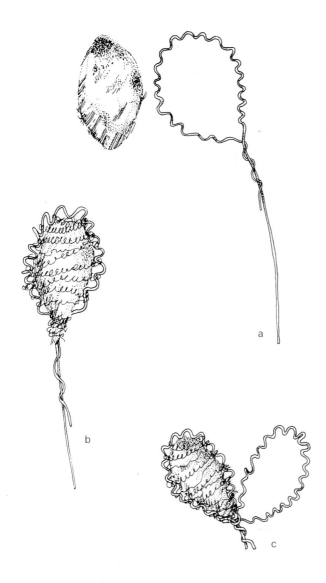

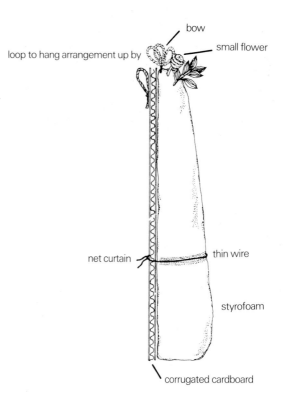

25 Making a cone to insert flowers into

24 Making a wire flower. The steel wire is wound spirally round a knitting needle. The spiral is then bent into an oval leaf shape (a) and a piece of velvet or gold brocade secured using a length of gold wire (b). Further leaves can then be added to the main stem as desired (c).

are later used for gold bows or velvet loops on wire (fig. 27). Lower down there is a bow and some gold leaves cut out of foil. In the middle we insert some wired roses (fig. 28). The aniseed stars and the beech-nut pods are first decorated with a blue or gold bead in the middle (fig. 29). It is not possible to give a hard and fast plan. Everyone will work with the materials they have, and in accordance with their own ideas of what is attractive. An arrangement like this grows like a crystal and the result will surprise its maker.

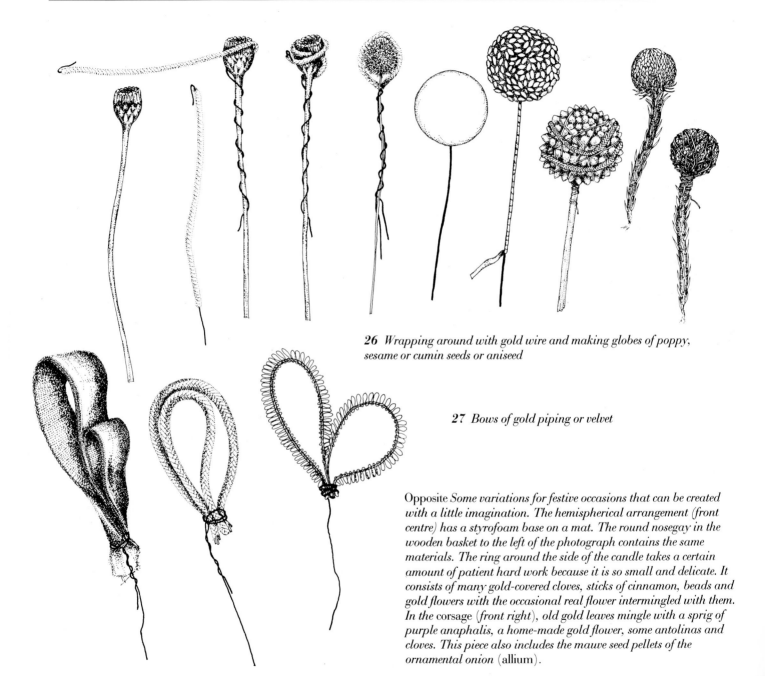

26 *Wrapping around with gold wire and making globes of poppy, sesame or cumin seeds or aniseed*

27 *Bows of gold piping or velvet*

Opposite *Some variations for festive occasions that can be created with a little imagination. The hemispherical arrangement (front centre) has a styrofoam base on a mat. The round nosegay in the wooden basket to the left of the photograph contains the same materials. The ring around the side of the candle takes a certain amount of patient hard work because it is so small and delicate. It consists of many gold-covered cloves, sticks of cinnamon, beads and gold flowers with the occasional real flower intermingled with them. In the corsage (front right), old gold leaves mingle with a sprig of purple anaphalis, a home-made gold flower, some antolinas and cloves. This piece also includes the mauve seed pellets of the ornamental onion (allium).*

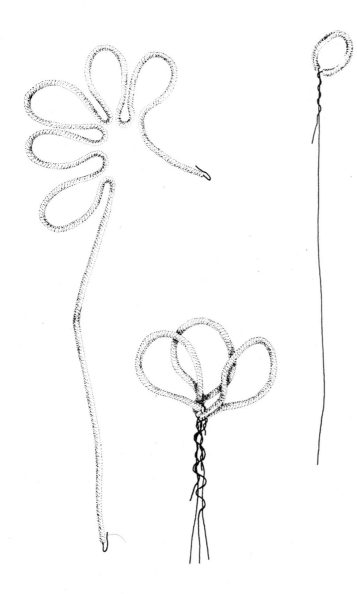

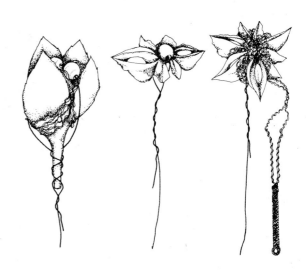

29 An aniseed star is decorated with a bead and unravelled gold spiral

We have tried to give a brief idea of the riches of nature that one can grow oneself, that can be bought as flower seeds, and that will make your rooms colourful at all seasons. At the same time, you are invited to experiment with what nature provides, whether found in the country or grown in the garden or window-box, on the garden table or the terrace. Paint alone will not enliven a room, and an arrangement of dried flowers in your bedroom means that the summer sun really never sets for you.

If success is not found immediately, you must bear in mind that in every experiment a failure teaches one as much as a success, provided one does not lose heart. And if things should go really badly, bear in mind the old saying, 'Who sows in sadness will reap in joy'.

28 Making roses from gold spiral piping

INDEX

Page numbers in *italics* refer to illustrations. Generally, only the common name of a plant is listed.

PROTECTED WILD PLANTS

The following is a list of plants that are protected by the Wildlife and Countryside Act 1981. It is illegal to pick, uproot, destroy or sell any of these plants; to collect or sell their seed; and to uproot any other wild plant (unless you are an authorized person).

Adder's tongue Spearwort   *Ranunculus ophioglossifolius*
Alpine Catchfly   *Lychnis alpina*
Alpine Gentian   *Gentiana nivalis*
Alpine Sow-thistle   *Cicerbita alpina*
Alpine Woodsia   *Woodsia alpina*
Bedstraw Broomrape   *Orobanche caryophyllacea*
Blue Heath   *Phyllodoce caerulea*
Bog Myrtle   *Mirica gale*
Brown Galingale   *Cyperus fuscus*
Cheddar Pink   *Dianthus gratianopolitanus*
Childling Pink   *Petrorhagia nanteuilii*
Diapensia   *Diapensia lapponica*
Dickie's Bladder-fern   *Cystopteris dickienana*
Downy Woundwort   *Stachys germanica*
Drooping Saxifrage   *Saxifraga cernua*
Early Spider-orchid   *Ophrys sphegodes*
Fen Orchid   *Liparis loeselii*
Fen Violet   *Viola persicifolia*
Field Cow-wheat   *Melampyrum arvense*
Field Eryngo   *Eryngium campestre*
Field Wormwood   *Artemista campestris*
Ghost Orchid   *Epipogium aphyllum*
Greater Yellow-rattle   *Rhinanthus serotinus*
Jersey Cudweed   *Gnaphalium luteoalbum*
Killarney Fern   *Trichomanes speciosum*
Lady's-slipper   *Cypripedium calceolus*
Late Spider-orchid   *Ophrys fuciflora*
Least Lettuce   *Lactuca saligna*

Limestone Woundwort   *Stachys alpina*
Lizard Orchid   *Himantoglossum hircinum*
Military Orchid   *Orchis militaris*
Monkey Orchid   *Orchis simia*
Norwegian Sandwort   *Arenaria norvegica*
Oblong Woodsia   *Woodsia ilvensis*
Oxtongue Broomrape   *Orobanche loricata*
Perennial Knawel   *Scleranthus perennis*
Plymouth Pear   *Pyrus cordata*
Purple Spurge   *Euphorbia peplis*
Red Helleborine   *Cephalanthera rubra*
Ribbon-leaved Water-plantain   *Alisma gramineum*
Rock Cinquefoil   *Potentilla rupestris*
Rock Sea-lavender (two rare species)
Limonium paradoxum/Limonium recurvum
Rough Marsh-mallow   *Althaea hirsuta*
Round-headed Leek   *Allium sphaerocephalon*
Sea Knotgrass   *Polygonum maritimum*
Sickle-leaved Hare's-ear   *Bupleurum falcatum*
Small Alison   *Alyssum alyssoides*
Small Hare's-ear   *Bupleurum baldense*
Snowdon Lily   *Lloydia serotina*
Spiked Speedwell   *Veronica spicata*
Spring Gentian   *Gentiana verna*
Starfruit   *Damasonium alisma*
Starved Wood-sedge   *Carex depauperata*
Teesdale Sandwort   *Minuartia stricta*
Thistle Broomrape   *Orobanche reticulata*
Triangular Club-rush   *Scirpus triquetrus*
Tufted Saxifrage   *Saxifraga cespitosa*
Water Germander   *Teucrium scordium*
Whorled Solomon's-seal   *Polygonatum verticillatum*
Wild Cotoneaster   *Cotoneaster integerrimus*
Wild Gladiolus   *Gladiolus illyricus*
Wood Calamint   *Calamintha sylvatica*